THE CLASSICIST

№10: 2012-2013

THE CLASSICIST AT LARGE 4

Re-inventing the Classical Urban Façade in Renaissance Rome

ESSAY 6

Traditional Collegiate Architecture in America:
A Timely Reassessment
Aaron M. Helfand

FROM THE OFFICES 28

ESSAY 42

Another Rome:
The Architecture and Urbanism of Armando Brasini
Steven W. Semes

FROM THE ACADEMIES 60

Anniversary Observations on Education at the ICAA
Paul Gunther

Notre Dame/Miami/Judson

THE ALLIED ARTS 82

Grand Central Academy of Art

MISCELLANEA 92

Table in Rome
Jana Vandergoot

Why the Classical?
Two Decades of Teaching at the University of Colorado
at Denver: A Retrospective Glance
Taisto H. Mäkelä

The Birth of the Grand Tour
Topographical Sketches and Descriptions
from Seventeenth-Century Rome
Claude Lorrain & Richard Lassels

ICAA Administration and Sponsors 116

HENRY HOPE REED, JR.
Champion of the Classical
Co-founder of Classical America 1968
Scholar-in-Residence,
Institute of Classical Architecture & Art 2003–13

1915–2013

There is such a quality as American taste and we will have to find it by looking to the best of our inheritance. The key to our future lies there.

The Classicist at Large
RE-INVENTING THE CLASSICAL URBAN FAÇADE IN RENAISSANCE ROME

Almost exactly six hundred years ago, while attending the Council of Constance (1414-1418), the Florentine humanist, Poggio Bracciolini made a momentous discovery in the nearby library of the monastery of St Gall: a copy of Vitruvius' *De architectura*, the only treatise on architecture to survive from the ancient world. While there is evidence to suggest that the treatise had already been known and occasionally used during the Middle Ages, this much vaunted "redis-covery" catapulted Vitruvius and his ideas to the forefront of the humanist project to revive antique culture in fif-teenth-century Italy.

Vitruvius' text on its own, however, was insufficient for a rebirth of classical architecture. First, the illustrations to which he referred in order to explain some of his more complicated concepts, such as entasis (the curvature applied to the taper of a column shaft) had not survived. Secondly, he peppered his Latin text with specialist Greek terms, a habit which reflected his reactionary attitude to the Augustan architecture of his own time but which made Leon Battista Alberti lament: "to the Latins he seems to write Greek, and to the Greeks, Latin: But indeed it is plain from the book itself, that he wrote neither Greek nor Latin, and he might almost as well have never wrote at all, at least with regard to us, since we cannot understand him" (IV.i, trans. J. Leoni). As we shall see, the Renaissance recovery of the classical tradition has a valuable lesson for the modern classical movement today.

Architects and theorists who wished to understand Vitruvius' treatise—and to see an *all'antica* classicism brought back to life—needed to supplement their study of the text with a careful analysis of the remains of ancient buildings. The problem was that the ancient building types which Vitruvius discussed and which could be found in Rome and other Italian towns—pagan temples, bath complexes, civic basilicas, theaters, and amphitheaters—were not the kinds of structures that fifteenth- and early sixteenth-century architects were being asked to design. These, for the most part, were churches, convents, hospitals, and, increasingly, the residential typology of the urban palace. To apply the classical orders to these new types of buildings a great deal of experimentation and innovation would be required.

The first patron in Rome to commission a classical palazzo was Cardinal Raffaele Riario who, not coin-cidentally, was also the dedicatee of the first printed edition of Vitruvius in 1486. Three years later the cardinal won a vast sum during a night of gambling and set about building Renaissance Rome's first *all'antica* residence for himself. The huge Palazzo Riario, or the Cancelleria as it is known today because it houses the Papal chancellery, drew on the talents of several architects including Bacio Pontelli, Antonio da Sangallo the Elder, and, when almost complete, Donato Bramante. The cliff-like travertine façade was articulated on the upper two stories by slender Corinthian pilasters thoughtfully arranged in a rhythmic sequence of alternating wide and narrow bays inspired by ancient triumphal arches. The result, though consciously neo-antique, failed in one important respect: It is difficult to believe that the pilasters are in any way related to the tectonic system that is actually providing support for the building. They are simply too thin and too widely spaced to represent a believable structure. In ancient Rome the classical orders had most prominently been used at a vast scale for public buildings such as temples and imperial baths, with column shafts often forty or even fifty feet tall. When these orders were reduced in scale to the floor heights of a residential building, even one as grand as Riario's palace where the piano nobile order was nearly nineteen feet tall, the shafts became very narrow, in this case only nineteen

Figure 1 (opposite page): Zecca (later Banco di Santo Spirito), Rome, by Antonio da Sangallo the Younger. Photograph by Jensens.

Figure 2 (left): Palazzo della Cancelleria, Rome, by Bacio Pontelli and others. Photograph by Lalupa.

Figure 3 (above): Palazzo Caprini, Rome, by Donato Bramante. Engraving by Antonio Lafreri, 1549.

inches wide. This resulted in pilasters that could not correspond visually to the load-bearing structure of the building and thus lacked the necessary gravitas to be convincingly neo-antique.

Bramante was keenly aware of this aesthetic failing in the facade of the Cancelleria and, in his own first commission for a palazzo in the city, clearly set about tackling the scale problem inherent in the application of the classical orders to a domestic typology. The Palazzo Caprini (c. 1501) was originally built for an official in the papal curia on a prominent site close to St. Peter's and later became Raphael's own house. Knowing that a single Corinthian pilaster scaled to the height of the piano nobile would look too skinny, Bramante instead articulated the façade with powerfully rusticated arches over which he set pairs of engaged Doric columns carrying the first triglyph frieze to be seen since antiquity. For such a small building the result is strikingly monumental.

Bramante's innovation of paired columns was clearly effective in addressing the fundamental challenge of this new Renaissance typology, but it was not accepted as the final word on the issue as we can see from the intense experimentation which occurred over the following three decades. All the major architects practicing in Rome before the Sack of the city in 1527 tried different solutions to the problem of applying the orders to an urban façade including, most notably, Baldassare Peruzzi at the Palazzo Ossoli-Missini (1517), Giulio Romano at the Palazzo Stati-Maccarani (1520), and Raphael at the Palazzetto Jacopo da Brescia (1515) and the Palazzo Alberini (1512-20). The attempt which was to prove most successful in the long run, however, was by Antonio da Sangallo the Younger at the Zecca, or Papal mint (1525). On the canted corner of a small triangular lot which faced the route of the famous Papal procession, the Possesso, Sangallo made a powerful architectural statement. With just three bays at his disposal he adopted a triumphal arch motif, but now scaled it up to the full height of the building. The resulting pilasters, which we call a "giant order" because they extend over more than one major story, now looked convincingly strong enough to actually support the building and were also appropriately scaled to the urban space in front. This motif was to prove hugely influential, initially being taken up by Michelangelo at the Campidoglio, and then becoming a recurring theme in palace design from Claude Perrault's East front of the Louvre (1667) to Sir Aston Webb's façade for Buckingham Palace (1913).

This account of the intense experimentation which was necessary to discover how to apply the classical orders to new building types in early sixteenth-century Rome, has a direct relevance to a similar challenge today: How to design the large scale urban façade such as that needed for the mid-rise office or apartment buildings that are essential to a truly sustainable city. There are a few excellent early twentieth-century examples of these types that draw on the Renaissance precedents discussed above—Lutyens' Britannic House (1924) for one—but we seem to have forgotten the invaluable techniques which the classical language offers for articulating a large multi-story façade with an appropriate sense of scale for its urban context; in particular, how to visually unite several stories at once through the use of giant orders, rusticated bases, attic stories, and the carefully placement of string and belt courses. It is vital that the tradition which has been continuously explored and expanded since Vitruvius was rediscovered six hundred years ago—and which we see in the inspiring work published in this tenth volume of *The Classicist*—needs to progress still further if it is to play a part in solving the pressing contemporary need to revitalize our towns and cities in a humane and sensitive manner. —RTJ

Traditional Collegiate Architecture in America
A TIMELY REASSESSMENT

By Aaron M. Helfand

The early decades of the twentieth century witnessed an unprecedented expansion in American institutions of higher education. In particular, the local or regional colleges of the Northeast with their colonial foundation experienced a transformation that would rival universities of international prominence. Corresponding with this increase in size and stature, these institutions embarked on ambitious building campaigns in order to accommodate their growing student bodies. It is the architectural manifestation of this collegiate transformation and its legacy in contemporary practice that forms the subject of this essay.

Many universities, in search of an appropriate architectural expression for institutional identity, opted for some variant of the "collegiate Gothic" style, thereby aligning themselves with the cultural and academic prestige of the medieval English universities. Across the country, hundreds of dormitories, classroom buildings, science labs, and other academic buildings were being constructed in stone or brick with Gothic and Tudor detailing. A few universities, notably Harvard, Yale, Princeton, and the University of Pennsylvania, went beyond mere stylistic emulation and attempted to recreate the organizational format of Cambridge and Oxford by introducing a collegiate residential system. This reorganization had several goals. First, by subdividing the student body into smaller social units, these institutions hoped to reinforce the sense of intimacy and community that was threatened by the overall increase in the size of the school.[1] Secondly, they sought to counteract divisions based on academic or extra-curricular interests, or more importantly, those based on social class, such as tended to be reinforced by fraternities and other private clubs.[2] Lastly, they sought to establish an academic and cultural approach similar to the ancient English universities. Oxford and Cambridge were widely admired by American academics and university administrators, many of whom worried that American

universities were beginning to place too much emphasis on research (in the manner of German universities), at the expense of teaching, which still held a central role in England. The social interaction of students and faculty who lived together within Oxbridge colleges was seen as a critical component of successful teaching.[3]

Although many of the buildings to be discussed here are Gothic, the scope of investigation is defined less by style than by the application of the collegiate format: a subdivision of the student body into smaller residential units, comprised of student and faculty accommodations arranged around courtyards with their own dining halls, libraries, common rooms, and other communal spaces.

The scale of these projects was unprecedented. Accommodating several hundred students each, at least fifteen new "colleges" or "houses" were completed at Harvard, Yale, and Princeton between 1910 and 1940. These buildings doubled the size of the Harvard and Yale campuses, while Princeton was completely transformed by its new Collegiate Gothic building campaign. Indeed, little effort was made to diminish the impact of these enormous new constructions. They were built in central locations and designed to be architecturally prominent, often featuring cupolas, towers, and other high-profile elements, which were immediately celebrated as the dominant architectural icons of their respective institutions. In this respect, they remain largely unsurpassed today.

Despite the magnitude of these projects, they have received relatively little attention in architectural history surveys, where they are frequently

Opposite: James Gamble Rogers, Harkness Tower, Yale University. Photograph by Aidan Wakely-Mulroney.

Figure 1 (above): Portrait of Ralph Adams Cram, 1911. Photograph by Theodore Marceau (Prints and Photographs Division, Library of Congress).

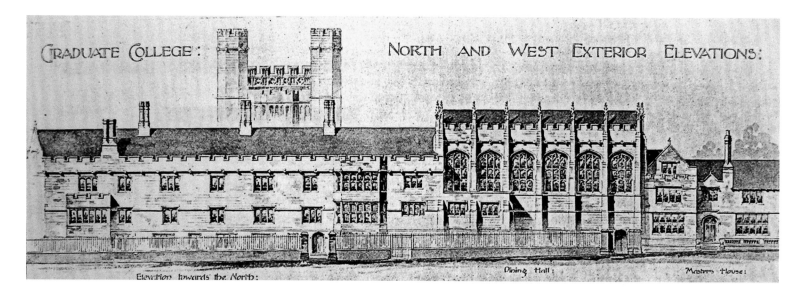

Graduate College: North and West Exterior Elevations:
Elevation towards the North: Dining Hall: Masters House:

dismissed if not completely neglected. Works focusing exclusively on the development of the Modernist style are likely to make only passing reference to anything not directly contributing to the development of that style.[4] In surveys of American architecture that at least touch on these works, they frequently do so with open contempt: Leland Roth, for example, devotes a single sentence to twentieth-century collegiate architecture, taking an attitude best summarized by his chapter heading "Nostalgia and the Avant-Garde, 1915-1940."[5] Similarly, David Handlin made the astonishingly improbable assertion that traditional styles were adopted over Modernism as a way of streamlining the design process.[6] This highlights a pervasive notion, and one that I will challenge here, that non-Modernist architects of the early twentieth century were merely copying old designs without innovation or adaptation. For instance, Marcus Whiffen and Frederick Koeper claimed that "[Ralph Adams] Cram's proclaimed disdain of copybook Gothic and pretensions to progressive developments are contradicted by his late work…his refectory for the Graduate College of Princeton, completed in 1913, while spatially magnificent, merely reproduces at a larger scale the dining halls of Oxford or Cambridge."[7] Ignoring for a moment the impossibility of a singular refectory at Princeton "reproducing" dozens of widely varying halls at Cambridge and Oxford, Whiffen's and Koeper's essential position is clear enough—that the collegiate architecture of the early twentieth century is derivative, and therefore hardly worthy of study.[8]

One might expect to find a more sympathetic assessment of these works in monographs dedicated exclusively to Gothic Revival in America, but even in this context twentieth-century collegiate work is perceived as lacking vitality and creativity. Wayne Andrews makes a brief mention of twentieth-century collegiate architecture in the final chapter of his survey, tellingly entitled "Gothic Dusk," a broadly critical review of Cram, who, he believes, found "painstaking reproduction of medieval trappings [to be] infinitely preferable to any invention."[9]

The prevailing critique of early-twentieth-century collegiate architecture is thought to fail on two counts: First, as derivative, lacking the creativity and invention of earlier eras and second, as ultimately inconsequential, due to what Andrews characterizes as the "complete triumph" of Modernism,[10] which for many decades left this generation of buildings without any identifiable architectural progeny. These twin claims may account for the relative neglect of twentieth-century American collegiate buildings in the study of Western architectural history.

In order to refute the criticisms outlined above, it will be useful to look at these buildings in terms of several principal themes. To assess the first claim, I will examine the ways in which medieval English precedents were adapted to the twentieth-century American context, as well as the ways in which twentieth-century buildings transformed and even surpassed those precedents. For the second claim, I will take into account a phenomenon, perhaps unforeseeable to many of the authors cited above: the resurgence of collegiate architecture in America since the beginning of the twenty-first century.

Ralph Adam Cram's Graduate College at Princeton and James Gamble Rogers' residential colleges at Yale are particularly relevant to the present study for several reasons. Firstly, they share the qualities of being both typologically and stylistically linked to their medieval English prototypes. (Harvard's river houses, for example, share the collegiate format but are stylistically more remote, while the Universities of Pennsylvania and Chicago display a close stylistic relationship but are less comparable in terms of scale and arrangement.) Secondly, they provide a useful comparison between urban and rural contexts, and are to that extent representative of other American institutions. Thirdly, each has commissioned a major new project: Princeton recently completed Whitman College, designed by Demetri Porphyrios, and Yale is about to commence construction on two new residential colleges, designed by Robert A. M. Stern. In each case, both work uniquely and intricately with the tradition of the twentieth-century works already anchoring these collegiate environments.

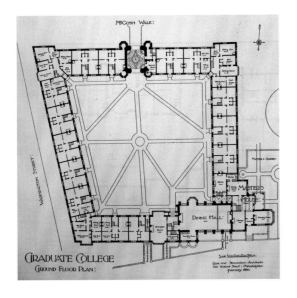

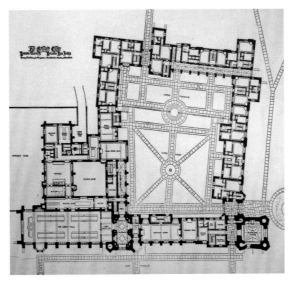

Ralph Adams Cram at Princeton: The Graduate College

In 1907, Ralph Adams Cram was appointed "supervising architect" at Princeton University, then in the midst of a major expansion campaign [Figure 1]. His role in this capacity was extensive: he was to provide "constant supervision and advice regarding the work of the architects actively employed and regarding the physical relation of the buildings to each other in the general material development of the University."[11] The University trustees had decided in 1896, with what Cram later characterized as "a wisdom beyond their generation,"[12] to mandate that all future buildings at Princeton be designed in a coordinated Gothic style. Among the first buildings of this campaign was a new graduate college designed in 1896 by Cope & Stewardson. Here Trinity College, Cambridge, provided the basic library of forms, all of which were subtly refined and arranged into a coherent new composition. The proposed graduate college was conceived not merely as a dormitory, but as a complete residential complex, with many of the defining elements of a medieval English college: student sets, Master's Lodge, dining hall, and kitchens, all arranged around an enclosed courtyard [Figure 2 and 3].

Although this early scheme was never completed, the concept provided the starting point for Cram when the project was revived in 1907. Cram was devoted to the Gothic style, especially in ecclesiastical and academic contexts, believing it to be nothing less than "the most perfect style ever devised by man."[13] It is perhaps not surprising, then, that he greatly admired the work of Cope & Stewardson, and sought to pick up where they had left off, commenting in his autobiography that "it was that very distinguished firm...that began the redemption of Princeton architecture... In succession to this firm, I was practically given a mandate to see that their work, so nobly begun, was completed."[14]

Despite Cram's admiration for Cope & Stewardson and his determination to continue designing in a similar style, his version of the Graduate College has a very different character from the original proposal. The most important difference is that, contrary to the assertions of Whiffen and Koeper, it is not possible to discern in Cram's designs any particular historical precedent for a given component; his approach was an equally knowledgeable yet less specific emulation of medieval architecture. Secondly, he brings to the design a concern for the picturesque, which he achieves through a variety of strategies.

It is useful at this point to address an issue that was the source of much debate at Princeton regarding the proposed location of the Graduate College. This discussion may at first seem tangential, but it provides some important insights into the weight given to English precedents in the course of the design process. The original location proposed for the new building was near the center of the campus, bounded on the east by Washington Street, and on the west by the old chapel. This site was championed by Princeton's President, Woodrow Wilson, on the grounds that the center of graduate study should be a visible presence in the university and continual inspiration to undergraduates. Cram supported this argument initially, and drew up his first scheme for the college on that location. However, the first Dean of the Graduate College, Andrew West, preferred a more spacious and secluded site a half-mile removed from the main campus.[15] He was joined in this preference by some alumni who lamented what they considered to be the over-building of Princeton's historically pastoral campus.[16] To allay these concerns, Cram turned to the example offered by Oxford and Cambridge. The *Princeton Alumni Weekly* from December 1908 describes a talk Cram delivered to an alumni gathering in New York, in which he addressed the debate on siting:

> *[Cram] showed a most interesting view combining a map of Oxford University and the new plan for Princeton on the same slide and at the same scale, illustrating, he said, how little basis there was for the criticisms which have been heard against the new plan to the effect that it would result in crowding and a loss of air and light. He pointed out that the contrasted plan showed instantly that the scale of the buildings, with their courts, quadrangles and intervening spaces, was much larger in every way than exists at Oxford, and he declared that—enforcing it by detailed plans of the various Oxford Colleges—Oxford still remained the most beautiful, spacious, and thoroughly scholastic educational environment in the world.*

A large number of views of the Oxford and Cambridge Colleges then followed, with a dissertation on the psychological importance of plan and style. Mr. Cram showed how the sheer beauty of Oxford and Cambridge formed one of the most potent influences in the cultural development of the student...[17]

What is important here is the way in which Oxford and Cambridge were held up as ideal paradigms for the physical qualities of a university, and the care that Cram took in studying the dimensions and proportions of Oxbridge colleges before laying out his own designs. He was careful to point out that Princeton's campus, even with the new buildings, would still be more spacious than its medieval ancestors. This argument, however, may have been geared towards comforting sceptical alumni. Cram himself seemed to welcome the increased density, which created a scale of open space more in line with the compact versions found in Oxford and Cambridge.

Cram was not responsible for the ultimate decision to build the Graduate College in the more remote location, and while he may have preferred the initial site, the new one offered him a great deal of flexibility. In fact, he described it as "the most spacious opportunity the office ever has had for working out its, by then, fully established ideas and principles in the matter of "Collegiate Gothic" adapted to contemporary conditions."[18] Notably, even without being limited by a confined or irregular site, he opted for an irregular and picturesque composition [FIGURE 4]. In this regard his design goes much further than that of Cope & Stewardson. This must be considered, therefore, a central part

Figure 5 (above): Ralph Adams Cram, 1926 proposal for the Graduate College, Princeton University (Cram and Ferguson Collection, courtesy of the Fine Arts Department, Boston Public Library, and Cram & Ferguson Architects).

Figure 6 (opposite right): J. M. W. Turner, Watercolor of Magdalen Tower and Bridge, Oxford. ©Trustees of the British Museum.

Figure 7 (opposite left): Ralph Adams Cram, Cleveland Memorial Tower, Graduate College, Princeton. Photograph by Aaron Helfand.

of Cram's strategy for capturing the aesthetic spirit of his English precedents; eccentric as the result of an accumulation of buildings, fitted into irregularly-shaped sites by many different designers in various styles over several centuries.

Ironically, this lack of rational planning or stylistic consistency, which resulted in the supposedly ideal Oxbridge models, is the very thing that Cram criticizes about the development of American campuses in the nineteenth century. Speaking to the Royal Institute of British Architects in 1912 on the subject of American university architecture, he complains:

...Our colleges are like Topsy, they "just growed," without rhyme or reason, subject to the most vacillating fashion and the quaint whims of emancipated individuals, and the results were generally shocking. In the plan of Princeton, as it was when I was put in charge, you will easily see how lawless had been the growth, and conditions were even worse at Harvard and Yale.[19]

His disdain for stylistic diversity is certainly born out by his work. Although he designed numerous buildings in the Georgian style (for example, at Williams College and Philips Exeter Academy), he took care never to mix Gothic and Georgian in the same ensemble of buildings. It is more difficult, however, to discern his attitude towards planning (or lack thereof), and in fact he seemed to harbor conflicting views on the matter. On the one hand, his master plan for Princeton is notable for its attempt to create a strong central axis of symmetry, yet his plans for individual buildings, especially the Graduate College, display a much more picturesque composition, characterized by asymmetrical, almost casual massing and arrangement of features. He even went so far as to rotate certain portions of the complex by a few degrees, giving the impression that the complex had been added to over time. This attention to subtle compositional refinements continued to be in evidence, when several years later Cram was called on to add a second court. He wrote to Henry B. Thompson, Chairman of the Grounds and Buildings Committee: "I suggest taking advantage of the fall in grades to keep this new quadrangle as low as possible so that it will build up against the existing buildings, rather than entirely blocking them from the north."[20] This aspect is illustrated in a 1923 perspective sketch, which shows a complex massing, enlivened by non-uniform roof heights and the introduction of gables, dormers, and chimneys of various types. The application of these elements becomes more intensified in a revised 1926 version [FIGURE 5]. The result of these design strategies is a college that, while stylistically coherent, gives the impression of being an almost organic accumulation of many smaller buildings, rather than a single monument.

The picturesque quality of Cram's design is facilitated by the fact that, like Cope & Stewardson's scheme, it is comprised of a number of distinct components, each of which are treated with a degree of formal autonomy. The elements are typical of English medieval colleges: student sets, common rooms, dining hall, kitchen, and even a large tower (serving here as a monument to Grover Cleveland). Unlike Cope & Stewardson's designs, and despite claims to the contrary noted earlier, none of the components of Cram's Graduate College derive from a single

identifiable source. Cram was explicit that "in point of style, no particular precedent was followed,"[21] and this assertion is born out by an examination of the building.

The prominence of Cleveland Tower within the collegiate ensemble has led a number of commentators, both then and now, to draw comparisons with that of Magdalen College, Oxford [FIGURE 6]. On the College's completion, for example, the *Princeton Alumni Weekly* commented: "The court is dominated by a lofty tower of such beauty of design that we can only compare it with that of Magdalen College, Oxford."[22] More recently, Raymond Rhinehart's *Campus Guide* characterizes the tower as "echoing in broad outline Oxford's Magdalen Tower."[23] However, within the context of Gothic towers, the only similarity is that the Cleveland Tower makes use of polygonal corner turrets, rather than the perhaps more common perpendicular or angled buttresses [FIGURE 7]. In fact, as *Architectural Record* was observant enough to note in 1914, "It is an exceptionally interesting study, for the reason that it is in exact conformity with no similar tower of the past."[24] The paired arches of Magdalen were reconsidered as triple arches at Princeton, with this tripartition carried down almost to its base (though not upwards into secondary pinnacles, as at Magdalen). All elements exhibit a more gradual and sophisticated tapering as they rise,

a refinement which is particularly pleasing in the pinnacles, making those of Magdalen seem almost mushroom-shaped by comparison [FIGURE 8]. Perhaps most unusually, the corner turrets are hexagonal rather than octagonal, a geometry which Cram found to be "supple and not only more effective in the resulting light and shade, but blessed with an almost psychic quality in these effects."[25] And, significantly, the Cleveland Tower is considerably larger than Magdalen's. On the whole, Cram succeeded in creating a design that evokes the celebrated model but surpasses it in scale, detail, and refinement.

A similar pattern may be observed in the Dining Hall, where the spectacular hammerbeam roof was designed as a variant of that found at Westminster Hall, London (rather than any Oxbridge College, as claimed by Whiffen and Koeper), yet more gracefully integrated with the windows, both along the sides and at the end of the hall [FIGURE 9]. The oriel window and the screen are elements characteristic of a collegiate hall, but each is more elaborate than any found in Oxford or Cambridge. Finally, the exterior of the hall, with its blunt corner turrets is entirely unprecedented among medieval English colleges [FIGURES 10 AND 11].

On completion, the Princeton Graduate College received universal praise from both the university and the architectural press. It was

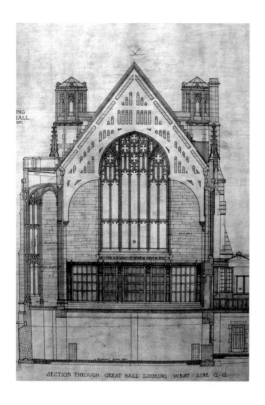

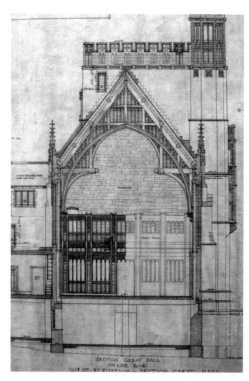

considered the crowning achievement of a generation of buildings (beginning with those of Cope & Stewardson) that far surpassed all of the University's previous architecture. The *Princeton Alumni Weekly* deemed the college "a triumph for the architect,"[26] while the *American Architect* hailed it as "the most exquisite example of Perpendicular Gothic that we have in this country."[27] *Architectural Record* favorably compared the new buildings to the old, claiming that, "unlike some universities, the older buildings at Princeton, even when they are *banal*, are at least inoffensive. They almost seem to serve as a background for the newer buildings, and their very lack of character prevents them from unpleasing conflict."[28]

These reviews attest to the success of Cram (and his contemporaries working at Princeton) in achieving their goal: a visually and spatially engaging, yet stylistically consistent ensemble of buildings, evocative of medieval English precedents, yet creatively responding to the demands and constraints of a modern American context.

JAMES GAMBLE ROGERS AT YALE:
THE RESIDENTIAL COLLEGES

The impact of James Gamble Rogers at Yale University was even more dramatic than that of Cram at Princeton [FIGURE 12]. His Yale commissions between 1921 and 1935 included eight residential colleges, the Sterling Memorial Library, the Law School, the Hall of Graduate Studies, the Yale Boathouse, the University Theatre, and several fraternity houses.[29] Of these projects, the most relevant to this dissertation are the residential colleges, although the Law School and Hall of Graduate Studies also conform, to an extent, to the collegiate format.

The building campaigns pursued by Princeton and Yale in these decades were similar in many regards. Both universities were interested in evoking the academic prestige, cultural associations, and aesthetic qualities of Oxford and Cambridge. Accordingly, as was the case at Princeton, Yale had decided as an institution to build consistently in the Gothic style, a decision that was made before Rogers was hired.[30] In the late 1920s, this interest in English models was taken a step further, when Edward Harkness made an unprecedented financial donation to the University in order to build a series of residential colleges for undergraduates. These were to be organized, like the Graduate College at Princeton (and their English predecessors), as enclosed courtyards with student rooms arranged in vertical entries and incorporating kitchens, dining halls, and common rooms.

Despite these similarities, though, the Yale colleges were to take on a distinctive character as a result of both their context and the attitude of their architect. Princeton's campus was rural and spacious (the Graduate College most of all), whereas Yale was located in the center of New Haven, a major New England city, with a grid plan that provided a significant challenge for any architect interested in the picturesque irregularities of medieval English architecture. But Rogers had a completely different outlook from Cram on the matter of style, and his eclectic tendencies in this regard allowed him to create a remarkably varied and playful ensemble of buildings, despite the limitations of their sites.

Although more liberal in his attitude towards style than Cram, Rogers' approach to specific historical precedents was perhaps closer to that of Cope & Stewardson. This is particularly notable in the first

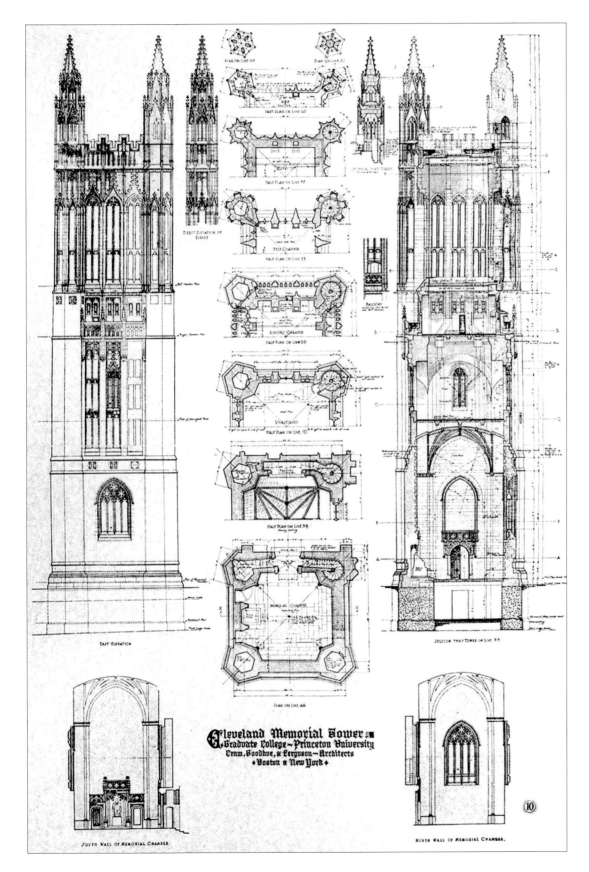

Figure 8 (left): Ralph Adams Cram, plan, section and elevation drawings for Cleveland Tower, Princeton Graduate College, from *The American Architect*, Vol. C, No. 1870.

Figure 9 (opposite right): Westminster Hall, London. Photograph by Ian Mansfield.

Figure 10 and 11 (opposite, left amd middle): Dining Hall, Graduate College, Princeton University (Cram and Ferguson Collection, courtesy of the Fine Arts Department, Boston Public Library, and Cram & Ferguson Architects).

Figure 12 (above): Portrait of James Gamble Rogers by Lawrie Lee. Photograph by Sage Ross.

dormitory group that Rogers designed for Yale, the Memorial Quadrangle of 1921 [OPENING FIGURE AND FIGURE 13]. Rogers subsequently renovated this complex, subdividing it into two distinct colleges (Branford and Saybrook), but the original design predated the implementation of the residential college system. Nevertheless, its overall form is strongly based on English medieval precedents. The complex is dominated by two towers: The Harkness Tower is recognizably inspired by the tower of St. Botolph's in Boston, England, while the Wrexham Tower is an explicit reference to St. Giles' in Wrexham, Wales [FIGURES 14-17]. Rogers, however, completely transformed his precedents in adapting them to their new context.

This transformation seems to have two primary motives. The first is Rogers' desire to improve on the aesthetic characteristics of his precedents. Rogers explained his attitude towards precedent in a set of notes he made for a potential book on the Memorial Quadrangle:

> To say that this tower is like any other tower is a mistake. In its original conception it was inspired from the Saint Botolph Tower in Boston, England, but the extreme thinness of that crown and the paucity of design demanded that considerable study and change be given it in order to secure a robustness that would give character and dignity.[31]

In an effort to refine St. Botolph's, Rogers added an extra octagonal tier to the Harkness Tower and subdivided the single large window of St. Botolph's into a pair of narrower windows; both moves contribute to the graceful tapering and upward thrust of the composition. Likewise, the pinnacles of the Wrexham tower are more delicately detailed and given a more attenuated proportion than those of their historical model. These are only the most prominent examples of such refinements in each design, which combine to give Rogers' towers an elegance surpassing their precedents.

These idealizations may be contrasted with a second type of modification, which derives from the interesting fact that both precedents are church-towers, engaged to buildings only on one side. They can, therefore, sustain a unified monumental treatment from top to bottom. Rogers' towers, however, are imbedded in residential ranges, each occurring at the intersection of three wings of varying heights. Thus, he modulated the scale and articulation of each tower towards their bases in order to integrate them visually with the rest of the Quadrangle. Rogers wrote that "we built [the Wrexham Tower] in the spirit only and when we made the details these were carried out to make a harmony with the whole group of buildings, in order to give it sentimental value without detracting from the beauty of the whole."[32] The resulting effect is of the towers emerging gradually and organically from the ensemble of buildings, rather than standing proud, like their ecclesiastical antecedents.[33]

The graceful lines of these towers lend them a certain sense of effortlessness, and it is perhaps this quality, combined with the existence of identifiable models that has led historians such as Handlin to suppose that such designs constituted little more than mindless copying,[34] the reproduction of historical forms for the sake of efficiency. Yet, a set of lecture notes from a talk Rogers gave on the subject of the Yale colleges reveals just how misleading such an impression is. The great challenge in designing a square tower with an octagonal top, he explained, was to proportion the octagon such that it "weaves" into the main body of the tower, rather than looking "like a pepper pot accidentally set on top." He wanted the pinnacles to align with the centres of the paired arches below, but this inevitably resulted in an irregular octagon. After numerous failed attempts to design a satisfactory octagonal crown for the tower, Rogers hired a designer who spent an entire winter attempting to work out the geometry at a cost of several thousand dollars. In the end, he presented ten designs, none of which were deemed satisfactory, leaving Rogers to ultimately find the solution himself.[35] This solution was "based on the principle of making a secondary crown with the points on the center line of the normal to each of the sides of an irregular octagon."[36] In other words, the lower octagon remains irregular in order to align with the arches below, while the upper octagon is rotated 22.5 degrees, allowing the pinnacles to be equidistant, thus forming a satisfactory crown. This degree of sophistication is simply not present in the original St. Botolph's, yet Rogers' significant improvement on the model has rarely been noted.[37]

One further point should be made in connection with the two towers, and that has to do with the choice of precedents. It was noted above that unlike the academic precedents that inspired the monuments at Princeton—Trinity, Cambridge and, to a lesser degree, Magdalen, Oxford—Yale's towers were based on churches. It seems that this selection was not based on religious grounds, but was made in order to

GENERAL VIEW OF THE MEMORIAL QUADRANGLE

Figure 13 (above): View of the Memorial Quadrangle, Yale University, from Robert Dudley French, *A Guide to the Memorial Quadrangle at Yale* (New Haven: Yale University Press, 1931).

Figure 14 (opposite top left): James Gamble Rogers, Harkness Tower, Yale University. Photograph by Ad Meskens.

Figure 15 (opposite top right): St Botolph's, Boston, UK. Photograph by Paul Stainthorp.

Figure 16 (opposite bottom left): Wrexham Tower, Yale University. Photograph by Aaron Helfand.

Figure 17 (opposite bottom right): St Giles, Wrexham. Photograph by David Powell.

infer certain symbolic connections with significant cities in Great Britain: Wrexham was suggested by the University's secretary, Anson Phelps Stokes, because of its connection with Elihu Yale,[38] while St. Botolph's was chosen, at least in part, because it was "a church rich in Puritan tradition, through its association with the name of the Reverend John Cotton."[39] In the end, formal considerations seem to have been the deciding factor. Rogers' notes state that "there [were] naturally many who did not care to have any other kind of tower than the usual four-pointed tower, similar to the Magdalen Tower that is used so often in this country, and even after this Harkness Tower was designed and modeled, we even went so far in considering this that we had a model made so we could show the tower both ways."[40] In any case, the adaptation of these two formally divergent, non-academic types to the Memorial Quadrangle reveals a greater eclecticism in the approach of Rogers, compared with that of Cram or Cope & Stewardson at Princeton.

This interest in formal variety and willingness to depart from academic precedent can be seen not just in the designs of these most prominent features, but as a recurring motif throughout the Yale colleges. As with Cram and others at Princeton, Rogers made the stylistic link with medieval England through the use of historically informed components, such as leaded casement windows, tracery, cusping, pinnacles, and Gothic molding profiles, all of which were assembled in creative ways to form novel picturesque compositions. The Memorial Quadrangle was in fact organized as not one but as a series of quadrangles of varying sizes: one large quad in the middle flanked by two medium ones to the east and three small ones to the west. By arranging the quadrangles in this asymmetrical fashion, Rogers began to relax the regularity of the rectangular site.

This irregularity was reinforced by Rogers' novel massing strategy. Quadrangles and courts at Oxford and Cambridge tended to be surrounded by buildings of a consistent height, but Rogers gradually modulated the building height from two-and-a-half stories at the south edge of the site to four-and-a-half at the north edge. Each court was thus bordered by a slightly lower building on its south side, a strategy

intended to introduce more sunlight into the courts.[41] The transitions from one height to another were handled in a variety of ways and were often used as an opportunity to introduce visual interest, through towers, turrets, and exposed gable ends.

These picturesque massing techniques were certainly exaggerated in comparison with medieval English models and were even more complex than those employed by Cram at Princeton. While Cram deliberately designed his Graduate College as several unequal courtyards, the variation in both area and height between the six courtyards of the Memorial Quadrangle afforded a far greater contrast in character from one courtyard to the next. But Rogers went further still, introducing a variety of both materials and even style to individualize the courtyards. For example, the small Linonia Court in the southernmost corner of the complex is of red brick, whereas the rest of the complex employs a variety of granite and sandstone. The selection of the stone itself involved the comparing of samples from at least 17 states and even some from Europe. Robert French writes "it was part of the architect's purpose to use a wide variety of material, choosing with a certain freedom as the old Gothic builders did."[42] (This may be compared to Cram's consistent use of local New Jersey stone for the Princeton Graduate College.)

In addition to the greater variation of material, Rogers reveled in the whimsical mixing of styles, which for Cram would have bordered on sacrilege. But, as pointed out earlier, the juxtaposition of contrasting styles was a hallmark of many of the English colleges that Yale and Princeton sought to evoke. Both Oxford and Cambridge are home to examples of transitional buildings of the sixteenth and seventeenth centuries, in which vestigial Gothic detailing is combined with the newly imported classical vocabulary of the Renaissance. At Cambridge, for instance, the Old Library (1624) at St. John's College and the Chapel (1628-32) at Peterhouse are quintessential examples [FIGURE 18]. There are numerous examples, as well, of Renaissance or Georgian modifications and additions to medieval buildings, such as may be seen at Jesus College, Oxford, or Trinity College, Cambridge.

Rogers clearly had no ideological or aesthetic preference for Gothic in the way that Cram had. In fact, his lecture notes reveal that he at first "felt Yale made [a] mistake choosing Gothic," although he changed his mind, and had come to favor "Gothic, [a] sprinkling of Georgian, Colonial, [and] some Renaissance, properly placed."[43] This eclectic attitude first manifests itself in the Memorial Quadrangle, which, although primarily Gothic, includes a number of classical Renaissance elements, including door surrounds and arcades. Some of these elements are treated as transitional Gothic-Renaissance designs, such as the door surround in FIGURE 19, which even introduces a whimsical early-Renaissance naïveté in the composition of the entablature and its misalignment with the pilasters. Other elements, such as the door surround in FIGURE 20, are more sophisticated classical designs, giving the impression of being later additions to a medieval building.

This penchant for mixing styles became even more pronounced in Rogers' later residential college designs. Of the six colleges he designed at Yale from 1932 to 1935, two are Gothic (Jonathan Edwards and Berkeley), one a sort of Romanesque (Trumbull), and three Georgian or Colonial in style (Timothy Dwight, Pierson, and Davenport). In

several cases, styles are mixed within the colleges as well. Trumbull, for example, introduced an ornate Gothic screen into its otherwise Romanesque dining hall. In Davenport we find Georgian and Greek Revival door surrounds side by side [FIGURES 21 AND 22], and in perhaps the most famous example, one of Davenport's ranges is brick Georgian on the courtyard and stone Gothic on the street side, where it faces the Memorial Quadrangle [FIGURES 23 AND 24].

These later residential colleges also display examples of the other picturesque strategies found in the Memorial Quadrangle. The massing is similarly varied, with northern ranges consistently higher by several stories than those on the southern side of the courtyards. Clearly, Rogers was interested in the potential for adding visual interest by mixing materials. A number of colleges switch from stone to brick, or from red brick to whitewashed brick. In Jonathan Edwards College, for example, the dynamic massing of the courtyard is accentuated by assigning contrasting materials to different blocks; the massing and fenestration on the long York Street façade remain relatively subdued and visual interest is created by the gradual transition from stone to brick, generating a patchwork texture again echoing Trinity College [FIGURE 25]. These playful masonry effects were not simply left up to the whims of the individual masons, but painstakingly detailed in construction drawings reviewed by the architect [FIGURE 26].

Such efforts certainly did not go unappreciated at the time. As was the case with Cram's buildings at Princeton, Rogers' works at Yale were instantly celebrated as masterpieces, surpassing anything previously built on that campus. Robert French's commemorative book on the Memorial Quadrangle, published in 1929, praised "its variety, its whimsical play of fancy, its sudden moments of austerity, its sympathy with all the ways and moods of youth…a unity born of many diverse personalities, like Yale herself…"[44] It is of interest to note that this inventive liveliness was not seen in opposition to, but rather in harmony with the design's grounding in historical precedent. French was equally effusive regarding the Memorial Quadrangle's allusions to medieval architecture: "In its very essence, the group of buildings which the architect was designing was the child of tradition. The Gothic order to which he was committed has always been a keeper of records, a teller of

Figure 18 (opposite): Chapel, Peterhouse, Cambridge. Photograph by Aaron Helfand.

Figures 19 and 20 (above): Door surrounds, Memorial Quadrangle, Yale University. Photographs by Aaron Helfand.

old tales."[45] These seemingly contradictory impulses of playfulness and tradition, youth and age, are reconciled by Stanley T. Williams, who, himself waxing lyrical, explained what he understood to be the essence of these new Gothic buildings. "When Amphion played, new stones took their places in the old wall, and became part of it, at once; there was not a 'new' nor 'old,' but the ancient city of Thebes, stronger and more beautiful. So the [Harkness] Tower rises through the mist of green of the ancient campus, and is not new nor old, but Yale."[46]

The architectural press was equally enthusiastic: the Harkness Tower graced the cover of *Architectural Record* in September of 1921, which proclaimed: "Yale, mindful of the nobler traditions, has expressed them in these great stone buildings. Even our devotion to truth and light (the *Lux et Veritas* inscribed over the main gateway) is quickened."[47] Like French, *Architectural Record* praised Rogers' work for its "unity in diversity,"[48] a recurring theme at Yale, which sets it apart from the more stylistically consistent work of Cram at Princeton.

We can discern a difference between the two architects in terms of their respective approaches to style and their attitudes towards the adaptation of specific architectural precedent. What we find in both, though, is a detailed familiarity with medieval English precedents combined with a creative ability to synthesize multiple precedents and adapt them to novel circumstances. This thoughtful and creative engagement with history is far from the mindless copying suggested by most recent historians, and through this process, both architects succeed in surpassing the models from which they drew inspiration.

It now remains to investigate the impact that these buildings have had on more recent projects. Have collegiate designs of the twenty-first century relied primarily on medieval sources, or were they influenced by works of the twentieth century? Has the institutional character that shaped the work of Cram and Rogers remained a significant influence on more recent projects? And, more importantly, what effect have Cram and Rogers had on today's designers?

DEMETRI PORPHYRIOS AT PRINCETON: WHITMAN COLLEGE

Although Princeton's Graduate College predated any of Yale's residential colleges, Princeton did not begin to establish residential colleges for undergraduates until the 1970s. By 1983, Princeton had created five such colleges, but only by retrofitting existing dormitories, rather than designing complete colleges from scratch. Thus, when Whitman College was founded in 2007, providing accommodation for 510 students, it was the first purpose-built residential college at Princeton since Cram's Graduate College was completed in 1913.

The architect chosen by the University, Dr. Demetri Porphyrios, is one of the leading figures in the late-twentieth-century renaissance of classical and traditional architecture. His stature within this movement can be gauged by the fact that he was the second recipient of the

Figure 21 and 22 (top left and right): Door surrounds, Davenport College, Yale University. Photographs by Aaron Helfand.

Figure 23 and 24 (middle left and right): James Gamble Rogers, Davenport College, Yale University. Photographs by Aaron Helfand.

Figure 25 (bottom left): James Gamble Rogers, Jonathan Edwards College, Yale University. Photograph by Aaron Helfand.

Figure 26 (opposite): Construction drawing, York St. Façade, Memorial Quadrangle, Yale University (Yale University Archives).

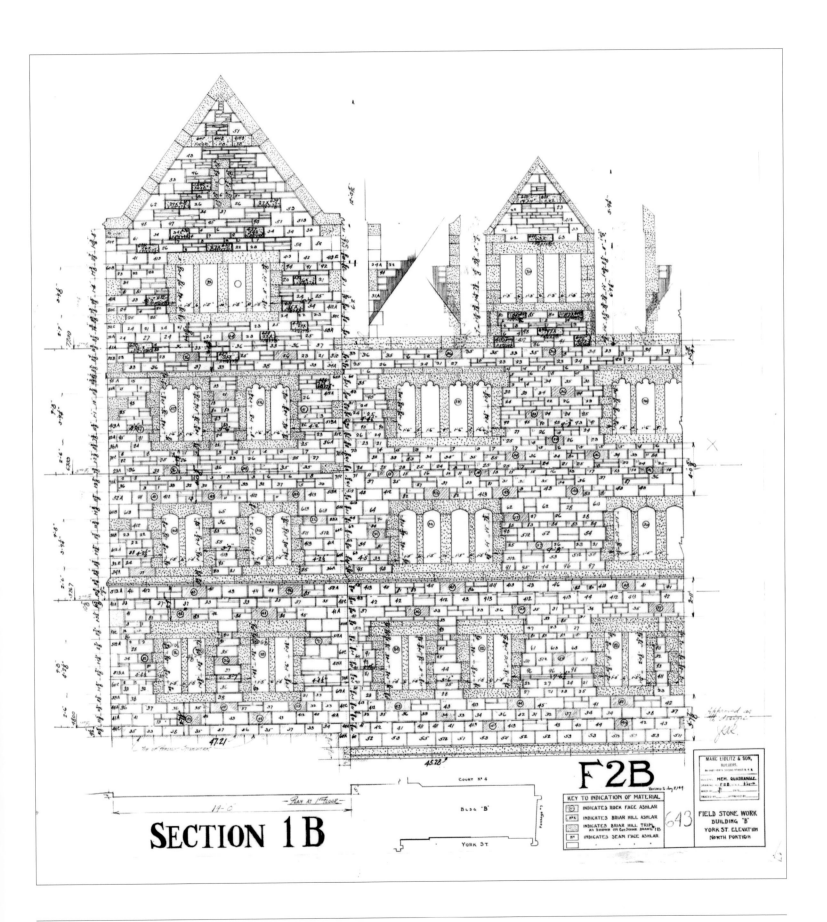

SECTION 1B

F2B

KEY TO INDICATION OF MATERIAL

INDICATES ROCK FACE ASHLAR
INDICATES BRIAR HILL ASHLAR
INDICATES BRIAR HILL TRIM
AS SHOWN ON CUT STONE DRAWING 1B
INDICATES SEAM FACE ASHLAR

FIELD STONE WORK
BUILDING "B"
YORK ST. ELEVATION
NORTH PORTION

Richard H. Driehaus Prize, established in 2003 to recognize excellence in classical architecture. Like Cram, his architectural output has been accompanied by substantial written work outlining his design philosophy. However, his views diverge from those of Cram. Whereas Cram prized traditional architecture for its cultural and religious connotations, Porphyrios is concerned more with its tectonic qualities. A central tenet of his philosophy is the notion that "classicism is not a style." In this view, the defining elements of classical architecture are its structural logic and the grammar that regulates the way in which its components are assembled.[49] Rather than divide architecture along stylistic labels, which he considers to be the "artificial product of architectural historians,"[50] he prefers to categorize architecture in terms of a spectrum from classical to vernacular. Cram considered the Gothic to be incompatible with Georgian, Beaux-Arts, or other branches of Greco-Roman classicism, a style with its own rules and patterns that, in fact, were superior to those of its stylistic competitors. Porphyrios, however, would go so far as to say that Gothic architecture is necessarily "vernacular, because its language is not sophisticated enough to develop an architectural grammar" in the way that Greco-Roman architecture does.[51]

Despite this philosophical divergence, Porphyrios' appreciation of Cram is highly evident, and his own design at Princeton turns out to be very closely linked to Cram's precedent. This connection is perhaps not as surprising as at first it seems. At the time Princeton hired Porphyrios to design its new residential college, its trustees had once again settled on a policy of employing Gothic architecture for its residential projects (if not for its academic buildings), seeking an architectural expression of the "values and culture of Princeton."[52] Porphyrios himself is a Princeton alumnus, having earned both his M.Arch. and his Ph.D.; while a graduate student, he resided for several years in Cram's Graduate College.

Porphyrios' intimate awareness of twentieth-century collegiate work at Princeton is balanced by a comparable familiarity with its medieval English antecedents. Working from his office in London, he has executed several commissions at Oxford and Cambridge, most notably the Grove Quadrangle at Magdalen College, Oxford, completed in 1998. Given this background, one may reasonably ask which precedents provided the dominant source of inspiration for Whitman College. Porphyrios explains that the University was eager for the new college to be not just a collegiate Gothic building, but "specifically a Princeton building, as opposed to a Yale building."[53] This distinction underscores the degree to which the diverging personal styles of Cram and Rogers had become identified with the institutions on which they worked. In order then to deliver a Princetonian design, Porphyrios had to look at the specific characteristics of Cram's collegiate style.

A close analysis of Whitman College, with the benefit of Porphyrios' commentary, reveals the extent of Cram's influence, even after almost a century. The most evident link is the overall organization of the college, which features two unequal courtyards, similar in size to the two main courtyards of the Graduate College. As with the Graduate College, the scale of the ranges is calibrated in proportion to the size of the courtyards. Notably, both of Porphyrios' courtyards are open on one side, a nod to the tradition established by Cope & Stewardson and Day & Klauder in Princeton's earlier undergraduate dormitories.

Like the Graduate College, Whitman is located on a large site unconstrained by other buildings, and similarly, the design takes advantage of this freedom, displaying a distinctly picturesque approach to massing and the disposition of its features. Porphyrios is careful, though, to point out the rational underpinning of what might at first seem to be arbitrary scenic moves. For example, the college is conscientiously subdivided into distinct buildings, since, as he explains, "the optimum size of a building doesn't necessarily match the size of the commission." In order to maintain a human scale and avoid monumentality, Porphyrios opted to conceive of Whitman College not as one large building, but as seven smaller buildings, arranged and connected in urbanistic terms. He pointed out that this approach had the advantage of being constructed incrementally if need be, and in turn offered a practical way of achieving the same visual effect present in an ancient college built over many centuries. To enhance this effect, and to enliven the ensemble, Porphyrios employed the same technique used by Cram of rotating certain buildings by a few degrees.[54]

Porphyrios was as equally attentive to details as to the overall organization and massing. The stone used is the same as that employed by Cram and others of his generation, and this material is instrumental in establishing a Princeton identity for the new college. Porphyrios, however, made greater use of the lighter-colored ashlar in order to highlight significant elements: the main gateway, the arcade, and the hall [FIGURE 28]. He identified certain motifs as typical of Princeton's earlier collegiate architecture, such as the grouped casement windows. He noted that these occur as single, double, triple or quadruple, but that in the last case, the central mullion is made heavier and is sometimes more elaborately carved. This strategy is used consistently throughout the College. However, just as Cram did not literally copy his precedents, Porphyrios did not slavishly adhere to Cram's model. Porphyrios points out, for example, that he has not followed the typical Princeton roof type, his being steeper. His windows are slightly larger than those typical of Cram's buildings.

The result of this balance is a college that could not be anywhere but Princeton, and one that cannot be mistaken for the work of Cram or his contemporaries. Perhaps the most striking difference at Whitman is its relative austerity in terms of ornament. Even as the level of architectural elaboration in most of the ranges is comparable to that found in Cram's work, the more honorific components, such as the gates, towers, and dining hall are greatly simplified, both in terms of carved stonework and in terms of the sculptural complexity of the massing. There are several factors that may account for this difference. Perhaps Porphyrios' view of Gothic as a vernacular mode of design restrained him from exploring the intricacies of Gothic ornament. Perhaps this is one facet of the design that reflects more medieval than twentieth-century precedents, as such simplicity is very much in keeping with what might be found in the earlier buildings at Oxford and Cambridge [FIGURE 29].

Almost certainly, though, economy was a critical factor. Although Whitman is lavish by today's standards, it is clear that a still greater

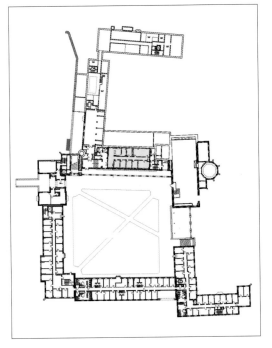

Figure 27 (far left): Plan, Whitman College, Princeton University.

Figure 28 (above): Demetri Porphyrios, Whitman College, Princeton University. Photograph by Aaron Helfand.

Figure 29 (left): Chapel, Jesus College, Cambridge. Photograph by Aaron Helfand.

expenditure would be required to support the level of craftsmanship required to produce carved ornament of a quantity found at the Graduate College. Furthermore, Porphyrios made the overall quality of construction a high priority in this project, which would have significantly diminished the resources available for ornamentation.[55] Most contemporary masonry buildings of this size are constructed as a steel frame from which is hung a two- to three-inch veneer of brick or stone, but Whitman College is unique in that the outer masonry is entirely self-supporting. In the conventional system, the masonry skin is connected to the frame at regular intervals by metal ties, which are liable to fail in a matter of decades.[56] By contrast, load-bearing masonry walls have a demonstrated ability to last centuries. Not only does this type of construction significantly increase the durability of the building, it allows the stones to be laid without regular expansion, which would otherwise compromise the visual integrity of the wall. According to Ellis Woodman's article on Whitman, the additional cost for load-bearing masonry construction was approximately $7,000,000, out of a total budget of $120,000,000. Thus, if the decision was between external opulence and long-term structural solidity, Porphyrios seems to have made the sensible choice.

Robert A. M. Stern at Yale: The New Residential Colleges

Yale has also recently embarked on a major building campaign, in this case for not one but two new residential colleges (provisionally referred to as the North and South Colleges), each housing approximately 425 undergraduates and jointly allowing Yale to expand its undergraduate student body by fifteen percent.[57] Although building has yet to begin, Robert A. M. Stern Architects has completed the construction documents for the project, and a number of highly detailed perspective renderings have been made which enable us to adequately compare the project to the completed work at Princeton and to earlier generations of collegiate architecture [Figure 30].

Just as Demetri Porphyrios proved an apt heir to the Princeton legacy of Cram, Robert A. M. Stern has been strongly influenced by the work of Rogers at Yale. The 2011 recipient of the Driehaus Prize himself, Stern has established what must be regarded as one of the most successful architectural practices in America today. As an author and as dean of the Yale School of Architecture (from which he received his M.Arch. in 1965), he has been an influential figure in academia as well as in practice. Like Rogers, he is known for his eclecticism, and does not share Porphyrios' qualms about thinking of architecture in stylistic terms. His projects span a wide range of styles, including Georgian, Tudor, vernacular colonial and shingle styles, and various strains of Modernism.

Yale hired Stern with the understanding that the new colleges would relate stylistically to the old colleges of Rogers, but of course, given the

diversity of styles incorporated into Rogers' work, Stern was left with a great degree of flexibility. Melissa DelVecchio, the partner leading the design team for the project, explains that Stern's decision to work primarily in Gothic reflects an assessment that despite the plurality of styles present in the old colleges, Gothic remains predominant and is the style most closely associated with Yale's campus as a whole. This is especially the case in the nearby Science Hill section of the campus. Furthermore, given that the site is somewhat removed from the other colleges, it was seen as essential that the towers of the new colleges form a visual link with the Harkness and Wrexham Towers, as well as that of the Hall of Graduate Studies, all of which are Gothic.[58] As will be discussed later, though, the issue of style in the new colleges is far more complex.

Like Porphyrios, Stern has both a familiarity with medieval collegiate architecture and a keen appreciation for the improvements made by twentieth-century American architects. In addition to his own extensive travels in England, Stern sent several members of the design team to Oxford and Cambridge at the beginning of the schematic design phase in order to study the architecture of the medieval colleges.[59] However, in his 1981 essay "Notes on Postmodernism," he is explicit about his preference for Yale's own collegiate architecture: "You can't go back to Cambridge or Oxford and see them fresh once you have been to [Yale's] Branford College. It's so much better at Branford; it's cleaned

---

Figure 30 (top right): Robert A. M. Stern Architects, Proposed new colleges, Yale University (Robert A. M. Stern Architects).

Figure 31 (bottom right): Robert A. M. Stern Architects, Elevation of Master's House (North College), Proposed new colleges, Yale University (Robert A. M. Stern Architects).

up, it's perfect, spatially regularized, marvelous."[60] This appreciation of the quality of Rogers' designs, combined with a strong desire to connect the new buildings with Yale's specific architectural character led Stern to draw primarily on intramural precedents. According to George de Brigard, an associate working on the project, precedent research was extensive, including visits to all of the residential colleges at Yale at the inception of each design phase. Furthermore, different groups were assigned to research and document specific details and elements from all of the colleges. Other American universities were studied as well, including the Princeton Graduate College, but as had been the case at Princeton, Yale administrators expressed a strong preference for their own buildings over those at other American universities.

These studies resulted in an extensive photographic catalogue of precedents, including specific sections on chimneys; windows and window surrounds; bay windows; passageways, gates, and doors; exterior lighting and decorative metalwork; gable ends; brick work; stone profiles; roof conditions; decorative stone elements; buttresses, moats and areaways; and elevations of Masters' houses. Each of these sets is comprised of a map showing the locations of the examples, several paragraphs of written conclusions, and many pages of photographs. The notes go into great detail regarding the range of conditions encountered. For example, a section on windows notes: "muntin detailing ranges between a generic grid, to diamond-patterned muntins, to muntins detailed with more organic and symbolic patterns and images. In newer buildings the grid and diamond pattern is most prevalent, while older buildings have more ornate window-work." Elevations of the new colleges demonstrate the degree to which this variety of window types has been incorporated into Stern's design.

The fact that the project is comprised of two distinct colleges presented an interesting question about its style, and the way in which the two colleges could be compatible yet retain distinctive identities. This problem closely echoes those faced by Rogers in the 1930s. Although Rogers' colleges may be said to emphasize stylistic diversity over compatibility, the distinction between Stern's new colleges is subtler. His preferred analogy for explaining the relationship is that the two colleges should be like "fraternal twins."[61] As twins, they employ the same palette of materials (red brick with stone trim) as well as a similar overall style. However, for the sake of differentiation, the two colleges have been designed by separate teams. This strategy is similar to that employed in Rogers' office, where the design for each college was overseen by a different associate.[62] At Stern's office, the two teams worked independently, but met regularly to coordinate the two designs. Certain motifs and strategies, such as particular dormer types, were reserved for one college or the other. Each college is made unique by particular individualized components, such as their libraries, dining halls, masters' houses, and towers. In this way, Stern is able to ensure an individual identity for each college, an important feature of the English collegiate tradition, and one that was carefully nurtured by Rogers in the first generation of Yale colleges.

Another hallmark of Rogers' approach that has been picked up by Stern is the playful mixing of styles. Stern's strategy in the new colleges may be most comparable to the Branford and Saybrook Colleges, formed out of the old Memorial Quadrangle, where the style is predominantly Gothic but flirts with early Renaissance classicism. Thus, classical details occasionally appear as door surrounds, gable ends, and other points of architectural elaboration [FIGURE 31].

In addition to these "Tudorbethan" highlights, Stern delves into a more sophisticated classicism, notably in the large tower of North College and in the dining halls. The phenomenon of a classical hall interior within a medieval shell is not uncommon at Oxford and Cambridge, where medieval halls were frequently remodeled in the eighteenth century. This can be found, for example, at St. John's College, Oxford, and Emmanuel College, Cambridge [FIGURE 32]. At Yale, Stern has introduced a bold classicism for both dining halls, especially in the South College, where the sculptural richness of the Elizabethan bays and the vaulted ceiling are enriched by inventive, almost Lutyens-like classical detailing [FIGURE 33]. The dining hall of the North College is somewhat more conventionally Georgian in character, yet with its own moments of invention, as in the subtly enlivened mullion pattern in the arched windows.

Perhaps the finest example of this sort of detailing is in the tower. As with Cram's Cleveland Tower and Rogers' Harkness Tower, the 190-foot tower of North College seems destined to become the defining hallmark of Stern's work at Yale [FIGURE 34]. The original idea called firmly for a Gothic tower; in the development of the design, however, it has undergone a classical translation, with echoes of Hawksmoor's All Souls College, Oxford [FIGURE 35] and St. Anne's Limehouse, London. The stone and brick shaft retains a Gothic verticality, yet it is crowned by a monumental, tiered lantern of round arches and classical finials. With this bold display of eclecticism, it will engage in a dynamic conversation with Yale's older towers, and perhaps most importantly, it will provide as memorable an icon for the new colleges as the older towers have for theirs.

CONCLUSION

We cannot yet know whether the new colleges of Porphyrios and Stern will be as influential a century from now as the colleges of Cram and Rogers have proven to be. What is clear, at least for now, is that the tradition of twentieth-century collegiate architecture is alive and well, fueled by a renewed knowledge of and respect for historical precedent and a drive towards creativity and invention.

Architects such as Robert Stern and Demetri Porphyrios have realized what most recent historians have failed to notice: rather than mindlessly copying medieval buildings, Cram, Rogers and others of their generation reinvented those examples through a process of synthesis, adaptation, and invention. By this process, Rogers transformed the "Boston Stump" into the soaring Harkness Tower, and Cram devised a dining hall that seemed to weave the grandest halls of Oxford, Cambridge, and Westminster into a single majestic space.

Although this approach to design has been deeply under-appreciated by historians for most of the last century, it is encouraging that institutions such as Yale and Princeton are now making such immense investments in projects that seek to reanimate this tradition. This investment is not without risks. Architects working in the early twentieth century benefited

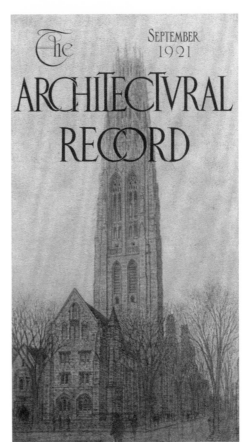

Figure 32 (opposite): Hall, Emmanuel College, Cambridge. Photograph by Aaron Helfand.

Figure 33 (top left): Robert A. M. Stern Architects, Dining Hall (South College), Proposed new colleges, Yale University (dbox for Robert A. M. Stern Architects).

Figure 34 (top right): Robert A. M. Stern Architects, Perspective, Proposed new colleges, Yale University (dbox for Robert A. M. Stern Architects).

Figure 35 (far left): All Soul's College, Oxford. Photograph by Tony Hisgett.

Figure 36 (left): Cover illustration of Harkness Tower, *Architectural Record,* September 1921.

from centuries of accumulated knowledge of the great architectural traditions, directly transmitted through apprenticeships and the academy. By contrast, due to the anti-traditional ideology of all but two or three architecture schools, the majority of today's designers have to discover and learn these traditions on their own. To design in a manner that invites comparison with the best examples of the past requires a degree of bravery on the part of both the architect and the client. Nonetheless, we are now seeing an increasing number of such projects, and their quality seems to be continually improving, aided by the close study of the techniques and strategies employed by similarly minded architects of the early twentieth century.

The challenges encountered by today's architects, as they seek to build upon the work of that earlier generation, should give both architects and historians a renewed appreciation for the skill required to successfully design within an established tradition. Yet, this tradition has remained relatively neglected by the architectural press and by academia in general. In comparison to the attention lavished on Rogers' and Cram's work by the architectural periodicals in the early twentieth century, very little has been written on Whitman College, and it remains to be seen whether Stern's imposing tower will appear on the cover of *Architectural Record* as the Harkness Tower did in 1921. [FIGURE 36]

A review of the literature covering architecture since 1900 suggests that this neglect is founded on the belief that the rise of Modernism succeeded in its attempt to make all other modes of design irrelevant. But rarely in history has the emergence of new forms resulted in the complete obsolescence of older idioms, and the recent projects by Porphyrios and Stern provide some of the strongest indicators yet that this remains the case. Although the extent of Modernism's influence in the twentieth century cannot be denied, there are some architectural goals that Modernism is ill-equipped to achieve, especially the establishment of local identity, the perpetuation of institutional traditions, and the forging of cultural connections and historical associations. These functions are of central importance for many institutions, not the least of which are schools, colleges, and universities. Where residential life is concerned, such considerations are critical to the establishment of a vital and cohesive community. Yale, Princeton, and many other academic institutions have once again come to this realization. It is up to architects to provide their clients with buildings that meet these needs and live up to the long tradition of design fostered by history's greatest architects. In turn, it is the responsibility of architectural critics and historians to ensure that such projects are fairly judged by the highest standards of the past. ✦

Aaron Helfand is an associate at Albert, Righter & Tittmann, Architects, Inc., and an instructor at Boston Architectural College.

NOTES

This essay is based on my M.Phil. dissertation completed at the University of Cambridge in 2011. I am indebted to a number of people for their help in the research and writing of this paper. I would like to thank the staff at every library and archive I visited during the course of my research, especially Cynthia Ostroff, Department of Manuscripts and Archives, Yale University Library; Christie Peterson, Mudd Library, Princeton University; Bill Whitaker and Nancy Miller, Architectural Archives, University of Pennsylvania; and Janice Chadbourne and Kim Tenny, Art Department, Boston Public Library. I would also like to thank Ethan Anthony, of Cram & Ferguson Architects, for making available to me the archives of Ralph Adams Cram. All images of the work of Ralph Adams Cram are used by permission of Cram & Ferguson Architects and all copyrights of such images are reserved to the firm. I am particularly grateful to Melissa DelVecchio and George de Brigard, of Robert A. M. Stern Architects, and to Dr. Demetri Porphyrios for their generosity in spending much time with me and for providing me with information and visual material relating to their recent and ongoing projects. For housing, feeding, and entertaining me during the course of my research in the United States, I would like to thank my friends, Noah Capurso and Allison Campbell, Brian and Maggie Saar, and Jordan Rodu, and my parents, Dr. Ira Helfand and Dr. Deborah Smith. I am grateful as well to my classmates, Max Bryant, Richard Butler, Otto Saumarez Smith, and Ben Wescoe, for reviewing and critiquing my drafts. Finally, I would like to extend my deepest thanks to my supervisor, Dr. Frank Salmon, for his help and support with this dissertation and throughout the course of my studies at Cambridge.

1 Paul Venable Turner, *Campus: An American Planning Tradition* (Cambridge, Mass: The MIT Press, 1984), pp. 215-216.

2 Harriet Hayes, *Planning Residence Halls for Undergraduate Students in American Colleges and Universities,* (New York: Teachers College, Columbia University, 1932), p. 66.

3 For a comprehensive discussion of the American adoption of English educational models, see: Alex Duke, *Importing Oxbridge: English Residential Colleges and American Universities* (New Haven: Yale University Press, 1996). This is also addressed in: Albert Bush-Brown, "Traditionalism and Progressivism," in *The New England Quarterly*, Vol. 25, No. 1 (Mar. 1952).

4 Kenneth Frampton, for example, takes only one sentence to acknowledge the limited application of the Modernist style in the first decades of the twentieth century, noting that that era exhibited "a sense of stylistic propriety…one style for the office, another for the suburban retreat, and still another for the idyll of the university…" Kenneth Frampton, *Modern Architecture: A Critical History* (London: Thames & Hudson, 1992), p. 220. Curtis is more explicit in defining the limited scope of his *Modern Architecture Since 1900*, explaining that "were this a book on the architecture of the entire twentieth century, instead of a study of the traditions of modern [sic] architecture in their cultural setting, it would be necessary to devote a number of chapters to such phenomena as the continuation of the Gothic revival well into the 1930s in the United States…" William J. R. Curtis, *Modern Architecture Since 1900* (London: Phaidon Ltd., 1996), p. 291. Even in texts without such stylistic blinkers, scarcely more attention is paid to these buildings: Marvin Trachtenberg and Isabelle Hyman's comprehensive *Architecture: From Pre-History to Post-Modernism* ends its substantive discussion of the Gothic Revival with G. G. Scott and Alfred Waterhouse in the 1870-80s, after which point the style is only of interest to the extent that it tends towards abstraction (Gaudi) or incorporates modern materials (Boileau). Marvin Trachtenberg and Isabelle Hyman, *Architecture: from Pre-History to Post-Modernism: The Western Tradition* (London: Academy Editions, 1986), p. 478. Spiro Kostof, similarly, gives no attention to Gothic style after the Victorian age, except for a brief mention of its application to skyscrapers. Spiro Kostof, *A History of Architecture: Settings & Ritual* (New York: Oxford University Press, 1995). The one notable exception to this pattern of neglect is David Watkin's *A History of Western Architecture*. David Watkin, *A History of Western Architecture* (London: Laurence King, 1995), p. 503.

5 Leland Roth, *American Architecture: A History* (Boulder, Colorado: Westview Press, 2001), p. 357.

6 According to Handlin, American universities in the 1920s "…no longer used Gothic and Georgian with any deep conviction about the appropriateness of these styles to creating a collegiate ambiance. These conventions instead were drawn upon mainly to please alumni and to enable the architect to proceed quickly with his work. In

retrospect, one has to admire, however grudgingly, the fact that so much tracery and so many carved pediments were churned out in so short a time, but with only a few notable exceptions, the detailing of this work was simply copied from standard books. There was also no sustained attempt to respond in the language of these buildings to the often unique sites they occupied or to the changes in scale that occurred when Georgian was extended to five stories or Gothic spread out over several acres." David P. Handlin, *American Architecture* (London: Thames & Hudson, 1985), pp. 177-178.

7 Marcus Whiffen and Frederick Koeper, *American Architecture: 1607-1976* (Cambridge, Mass: MIT Press, 1981), p. 289.

8 John Burchard and Albert Bushe-Brown take the criticism a degree further, claiming not just that these buildings were mindless copies, but that they were dishonest because they combined traditional stylistic elements with modern steel construction techniques. Moreover, they claim that by alluding to medieval traditions, the designs were incompatible with modern culture. Taking Yale as an example, they characterize the use of medieval English precedents as a "masquerade" and complain that "it occurred to no one to introduce a new way of life by a new architecture; perhaps the question did not even arise whether Yale undergraduates were any longer leading the lives of medieval Oxonians..." John Burchard and Albert Bush-Brown, *The Architecture of America: A Social and Cultural History* (London: Victor Gollancz Ltd., 1967), pp.412-413.

9 Wayne Andrews, *Gothic: Its Origins, Its Trials, Its Triumphs* (New York: Random House, 1975), p. 141.

10 *Ibid.*

11 Meeting minutes of the Committee of Grounds and Buildings, March 9, 1907, Princeton University Archives, AC120 Box 50, Folder 12.

12 Ralph Adams Cram, "Recent University Architecture in the United States," in *Journal of the Royal Institute of British Architects*, May, 1912, p. 501.

13 Cram, "Recent University Architecture in the United States," p. 498.

14 Ralph Adams Cram, *My Life in Architecture* (Boston: Little, Brown & Co., 1936), p. 144.

15 For a full discussion of this debate, see Willard Thorp, Minor Myers, Jr., and Jeremiah Stanton Finch, "The Princeton Graduate School, A History," in Alexander Leitch, *A Princeton Companion* (Princeton: University Press, 1978), pp. 224-226.

16 One alumnus commented, in response to the proposed new buildings, that "what we want for Princeton is not only more handsome buildings, but more space in which to see them." (*Princeton Alumni Weekly*, Vol. IX, No. 11, December 9, 1908).

17 *Ibid.*

18 Cram, *My Life in Architecture*, p. 121.

19 Cram, "Recent University Architecture in the United States," p. 503.

20 Letter from R. A. Cram to Henry B. Thompson, (Princeton University Archives: AC035 Grounds and Buildings – Technical Correspondence Box 11 Folder 5: Graduate College 1923-1926).

21 Cram, *My Life in Architecture*, p. 122.

22 *Princeton Alumni Weekly*, November 19, 1913.

23 Raymond P. Rhinehart, *The Campus Guide: Princeton University* (New York: Princeton Architectural Press, 2000), p. 134.

24 C. Matlack Price, "A Study in Scholastic Architecture: The Graduate College Group of Princeton University," in Architectural Record, Vol. XXXV, No. 1 (Jan. 1914). p. 12.

25 Cram, *My Life in Architecture*, p. 122.

26 *Princeton Alumni Weekly*, Nov. 19, 1913.

27 Carswell, Harold Thorp, "The Graduate College of Princeton University," in *The American Architect*, Vol. C, No. 1870 (Oct. 25, 1911). p. 171.

28 Price, in *Architectural Record*, Vol. XXXV, No. 1 (Jan. 1914). p. 2.

29 A complete catalogue of projects is found in Aaron Betsky, James *Gamble Rogers and the Architecture of Pragmatism* (Cambridge, MA: MIT Press, 1994), pp. 261-268.

30 *Ibid.*, p. 49.

31 Rogers, James Gamble, "Notes for potential book on the Memorial Quadrangle," James Gamble Roger Papers, Yale University Library Manuscripts Collection, Acc. 18-M-16, Group No. 396, Box 38, Folder 288. p. 47. Rogers is not alone in his critique of the tower's design. Pevsner, noting its incremental design process, complains: "One cannot overlook the fact that tier followed tier to changed plans, and if one covers with one's hand the upper stages, a more harmonious relation between church and steeple appears at once." Nikolaus Pevsner and John Harris, *Buildings of England: Lincolnshire* (Harmondsworth: Penguin Books, 1964), p. 464.

32 *Ibid.*, p. 46.

33 Interestingly, Cram's Cleveland Tower seems to follow the latter, however he mentions in his memoir that he believed the massing of the Graduate College would be improved by the addition of another quadrangle to the east, thereby making the tower a more "central and focal feature instead of standing, as it now does, at one angle of a mass of buildings..." Cram, *My Life in Architecture*, p. 123.

34 Handlin, *op. cit.*, pp. 177-178.

35 Rogers, James Gamble, *Lecture notes*, James Gamble Roger Papers, Yale University Library Manuscripts Collection, Acc. 18-M-16, Group No. 396, Box 38, Folder 288. p. 10.

36 Rogers, *Memorial Quadrangle book notes*, p. 50.

37 Even Susan Ryan, in her discussion of Rogers' precedents, fails to note this innovation, seeing instead only a more "streamlined" version of St. Botolph's, an effect she attributes to Rogers' "interest in the idea of modernizing historic styles." Susan Ryan, "The Architecture of James Gamble Rogers at Yale University," in *Perspecta*, Vol. 18 (1982), p. 29.

38 Rogers, Lecture notes. p. 9.

39 Stanley T. Williams, *The Memorial Quadrangle and Harkness Memorial Tower* (New Haven: Yale University Press, 1911), p. 9.

40 Rogers, *Memorial Quadrangle book notes*, p. 48.

41 Rogers, *Lecture notes*. p. 2.

42 Robert Dudley French, ed., *The Memorial Quadrangle: A Book About Yale*, (New Haven: Yale University Press, 1929), p. 105.

43 Rogers, *Lecture notes*, p. 2.

44 Robert Dudley French, ed., *The Memorial Quadrangle: A Book About Yale*, (New Haven: Yale University Press, 1929), p. 101.

45 *Ibid.*, p. 105.

46 Stanley T. Williams, *The Memorial Quadrangle and Harkness Memorial Tower* (New Haven: Yale University Press, 1911), p. 4.

47 Marrion Wilcox, "The Harkness Memorial Quadrangle at Yale," in *Architectural Record*, Vol. L No. 3 (Sep. 1921). p. 163.

48 *Ibid.* p. 164.

49 Demetri Porphyrios, *Classicism is not a Style* (New York: St. Martin's Press, 1982).

50 Author's interview with Demetri Porphyrios, May 6, 2011.

51 Ibid.

52 Porphyrios' characterization of the trustees' stance.

53 Porphyrios interview, May 6, 2011.

54 Porphyrios interview, May 6, 2011.

55 Ellis Woodman, "Porphyrios Associates' Princeton University Whitman Building," in *Building Design*, (Feb. 2008).

56 Porphyrios interview, May 6, 2011.

57 http://newresidentialcolleges.yale.edu

58 Author's interview with Melissa DelVecchio, partner, Robert A. M. Stern Architects, April 18, 2011.

59 Author's interview with George de Brigard, associate, Robert A. M. Stern, Architects, April 18, 2011.

60 Robert A. M. Stern, *Architecture on the Edge of Postmodernism: Collected Essays, 1964-1988* (New Haven: Yale University Press, 2009), p. 173.

61 DelVecchio interview, April 18, 2011.

62 Susan Ryan, *op. cit.*, p. 37.

From the Offices

Richard Economakis

South Bend, Indiana

CIVIC HALL
Cayalá, Guatemala

PROJECT TEAM:
Richard Economakis, *Design Architect;* Léon Krier, *Consulting Architect and Masterplanner;* Pedro Godoy and María Sánchez (Estudio Urbano), *Supervising Architects and Town Architects*

Léon Krier planned the town of Cayalá in 2003 with Pedro Godoy and María Sánchez of the Guatemala-based firm of Estudio Urbano for the local development company Grupo Cayalá. The scheme, the first phase of which is now complete, seeks to create a sustainable, mixed use, pedestrian-oriented environment, where buildings reinforce a sense of place and defer to the human scale. Commercial, residential, and other private buildings are invested with individual character in accordance with their particular site, program, and context, and at the same time contribute to the making of a continuous urban fabric. The consistency of scale, architectural expression, and materials allow the more elaborate public buildings and monuments to stand out as urban set-pieces, overturning the established practice of building isolated self-referential object-buildings regardless of use and location. The masterplan provides for three major public edifices: a tower by Krier, a church by Godoy and Sánchez, and a Civic Hall by Richard Economakis, which is the first of the three to be built.

The architecture of Cayalá embraces regional Spanish and indigenous traditions, which are employed creatively and adapted to a variety of contemporary building types. These include multi-story mixed-use apartments, commercial structures, public buildings (such as parking pavilions), cinema complexes, markets, and larger civic and sacred edifices. Elevations are typically plastered, with stone trim and moldings. Balconies are either wooden or employ decorative ironwork, and roofs are finished in traditional red tiles.

Commercial streets and squares are lined with colonnades recalling the characteristic wooden porticos of Spanish plazas in the New World.

The Civic Hall known as the Club Cayalá, is a large gabled structure with pyramidal steps, a pedimented portico, and octagonal cupola tower situated at the center of the town. The building comprises a large ceremonial hall placed above a row of street-level shops opening onto a covered arcade that lines the west side of the main street. Economakis' design makes reference to a number of regional precedents. For instance, the large steps of the portico evoke the forms of Mayan temples, in particular the complex of Santo Tomás at Chichicastenango, which combines a pre-Columbian pyramid and Spanish church; the octagonal tower with its crowning lantern alludes to traditional cupolas in the historic city of Antigua Guatemala; the corner windows are derived from a local custom of fenestrating the ends of urban blocks; while the octagonal windows along the east elevation recall the deep-set clerestories along the north façade of the old University of San Carlos Borromeo in Antigua. The entrance portico is slightly detached from the main building's volume in the manner of the porch of the Chapel of the Resurrection at Enskede, Stockholm, by Sigurd Lewerentz. The portico however, is treated less formally to evoke a traditional market pavilion. The portico's Corinthian capitals incorporate a maize motif—an important feature in Mayan iconography—modeled on Giuseppe Franzoni's corn capitals for the U.S. Capitol building and executed by a local sculptor, Maria Isabel Madris.

A two-story wooden pergola shades the west elevation of the Civic Hall, which affords dramatic views of Guatemala City and the volcanic landscape beyond. This feature is derived from the attenuated porticoes of late-19th-century resorts, especially that of the

Athenaeum in Chautauqua, in upstate New York, by William Worth Carlin. Besides their obvious reference to the Mayan temple type, the great steps in front of the hall at Cayalá are meant to be used as an occasional stage or theatrical cavea for outdoor events. As such, in November 2011 they were put to use as a stepped podium for the festivities celebrating the completion of the master plan's first phase.

Previous pages: The Paseo, Cayalá, Guatemala, with the Civic Hall (right) by Richard Economakis, surrounding buildings by Estudio Urbano (Pedro Godoy and María Sánchez) and Richard Economakis, and fountains by Léon Krier. Photography by Vicente A. Aguirre.

Above: Corn capital, U.S. Capitol, Washington, DC, by Giuseppe Franzoni. Photograph courtesy of the Architect of the Capitol.

All images are used by permission of Richard Economakis.

John B. Murray Architect, LLC
New York, New York

A New Farmhouse
Columbia County, New York

PROJECT TEAM:
John B. Murray

John B. Murray Architect, LLC, was fortunate to be asked to design this residence on a 200-acre farm property in the southern region of Columbia County, New York by clients who appreciate the unique character of the local agrarian landscape. A couple with two college-age daughters, they wanted a house pared to its essentials that would meet their programmatic needs lucidly and in an aesthetic language and at a scale appropriate to the region known for simple farmhouses and dairy barns. They wished for their house to evince an austere beauty evocative of past centuries and an architectural ethos that quietly celebrates simplicity, function, and modesty.

As the site contained no existing architecture to give cues to the design, a historically and architecturally plausible story was developed for the house. The original owner was conceived of as a Dutch farmer, practical and discreet, who built himself a modest fieldstone cottage in the late eighteenth century. As the farm prospered, his descendants, using a country builder, added a Federal-style farmhouse that joined to the original by a hyphen and, later, a separate kitchen house was added with a barn beyond.

In addition to reducing the massing by creating a composition that takes advantage of the sloping site, the design facilitated precisely enough space for a contemporary program: a stone guest house; a classic center-hall main block, with dining, living, and exercise rooms downstairs and a master suite and twin home offices above. The kitchen, mudroom, three-season porch, and family room (as well as two

upstairs bedrooms) are in the kitchen wing. Moreover, as the site receives unobstructed sunlight from every direction and has views of the Berkshire Hills to the north, the firm oriented the structure so as to maximize both.

From an architectural standpoint, the original farmer was kept in mind, remembering that he would have been an austere man who would not have exceeded his purpose: his house would thus evoke more Washington than Jefferson. The detailing, everywhere restrained, is hierarchical, with the more refined Federal elements—carved plaster cornices, entablatures above windows, poplar-paneled end walls, and thin, attenuated mantelpieces—in the main block. Simpler vernacular carpentry is found in the kitchen wing, and a rustic approach is featured in the stone house. Antique fixtures and structural elements, as well as contemporary craftwork, strictly follow historic precedent and nearly

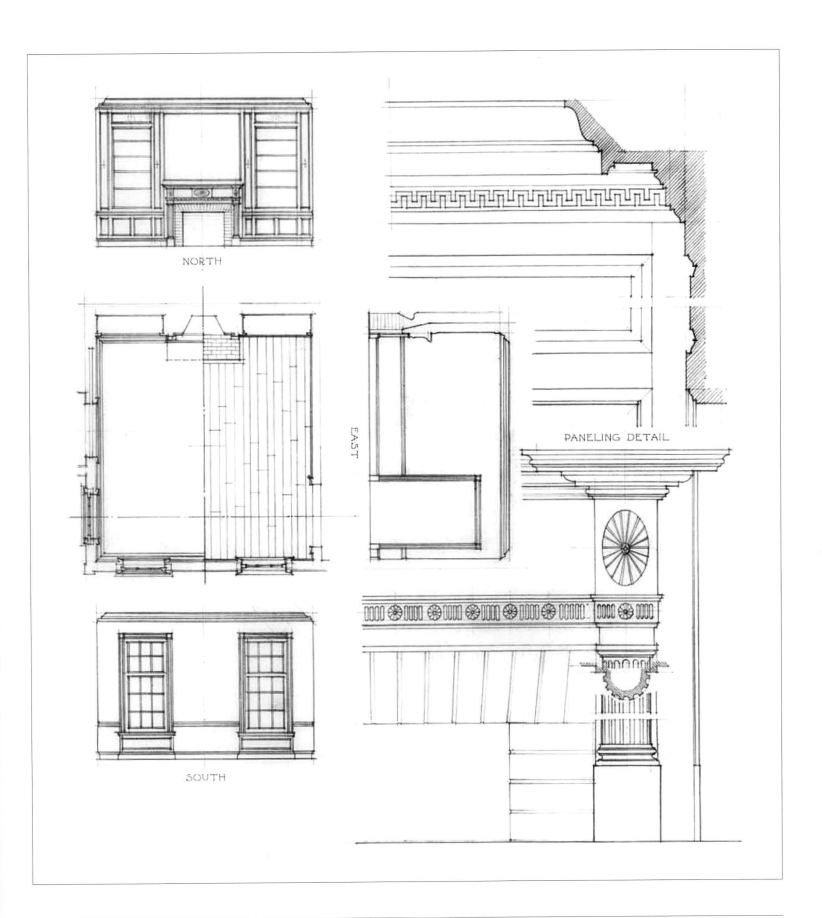

NORTH

EAST

PANELING DETAIL

SOUTH

every component remains authentic to the period (including the hand-hewn oak barn frame, which was rescued from a site in Buffalo).

The firm made two landscaping decisions that contribute significantly to the experience of the house. The first involved creating two terraced lawns, one behind the residence, the other beside the nearby pool, which domesticate the precincts adjacent to each and create a gentle buffer between the acres of working farmland and the more intimate realm of family life. The second, more impactful gesture was the siting of the entry drive alongside the hedgerow at the property's edge. Apart from avoiding the unnatural division of the fields, this route offers visitors an initial distant view of the house and then conceals it for much of the ensuing drive before finally revealing the house again upon arrival, a welcoming architectural presence.

The house's principal design challenges derived from opposing impulses: to make the structure as authentic to its period as possible, while also maximizing the residence's energy efficiency and installing the most contemporary mechanical, electrical, and communications systems. Making it old involved integrating antique architectural elements and building materials as well as using period-specific craft and construction techniques to build the house. As regards the former, 80 percent of the main wing's doors date from the Federal period, reclaimed lumber was used for the floors, and an antique mantelpiece was installed in the family room; all elements that imbue the residence with the spirit of early-nineteenth-century life in the Hudson Valley.

The embrace of historic craft techniques is perhaps most apparent in the laying up and dressing of the fieldstone walls of the Dutch wing. Multiple mock-ups were produced prior to construction and skilled stonemasons were engaged to execute the work. A comparable level of craft can be seen in the hand-carved mahogany handrail in the main house as well as in the newly made doors, which were built from salvaged boards carefully distressed to replicate the look of those from the period.

Like the handrail, the living room and master suite mantelpieces were hand-drawn in the studio using historic examples as models

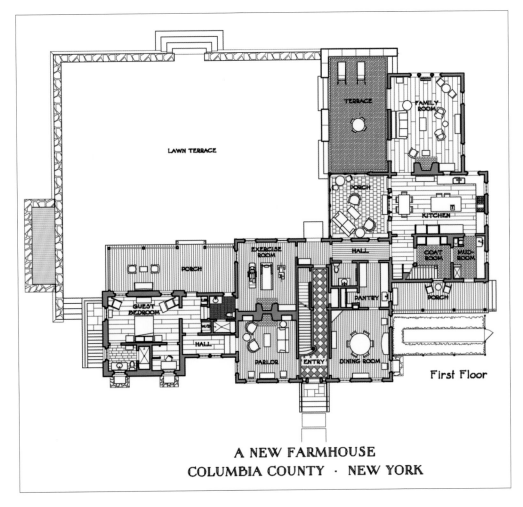

A NEW FARMHOUSE
COLUMBIA COUNTY · NEW YORK

First Floor

and constructed and finished with equal fidelity to the time. Research into Federal-era construction methods led to the use of cut nails to face-nail the floorboards and the rough-sawn beams in the family room. Hand-hewing might have conformed to today's notions of craft, but in fact that technique predates the house's epoch. Such details may seem minor, but ultimately made a difference in the way in which the residence is experienced.

The clients, despite their love of historic architecture, were very interested in making the house as energy efficient as possible, especially given Columbia County's sometimes-brutal winters. To this end, the studs in the house's two-by-six frame were staggered to prevent heat loss via conductivity between the interior and exterior walls and to allow the insertion of a continuous, unbroken blanket of foam insulation, a subtle construction adjustment that resulted in substantive energy savings.

Multiple gambits were used to disguise the elements that make this old house function in the modern world. The generator, transformer, and satellite dish are concealed behind the barn, and the compressors were buried in a stone pit that blends with the Dutch wing. And even the most austere eighteenth-century farmer would have given thanks for the snow-melt system in the walkway that connects the house and barn.

All images are used by permission of John B. Murray Architect, LLC.

McCrery Architects, LLC

Washington, District of Columbia

U.S. SUPREME COURT BOOKSTORE
Washington, District of Columbia

PROJECT TEAM:
Julia Garza; Elizabeth Ruedisale McNicholas

The Supreme Court Historical Society commissioned McCrery Architects to design a retail space in keeping with the outstanding architecture of Cass Gilbert's U.S. Supreme Court building. The sole contemporary space within the original historic Court building, it serves as a bookstore for the Justices' published works and as a gift shop for visitors to the Supreme Court. The robust design, with free-standing Greek Doric columns and a secondary order of Ionic pilasters, recalls the architecture of the original Supreme Court Chamber designed by Benjamin Henry Latrobe. The custom designed bookshelves, display cases, and sales counter are built from white oak, a species of wood selected to match the existing finishes elsewhere in the Court building.

All images are used by permission of McCrery Architects, LLC.

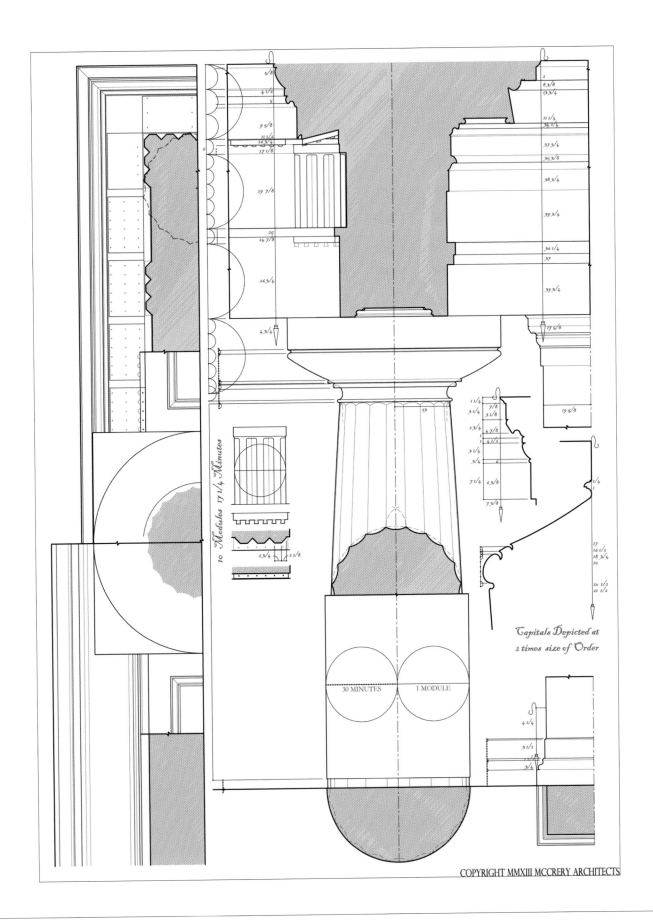

10 Modules 171/4 Minutes

Capitals Depicted at
2 times size of Order

30 MINUTES   1 MODULE

Eric J. Smith Architect

New York, New York

CALIFORNIA GEORGIAN
Atherton, California

PROJECT TEAM:
Eric J. Smith

This newly-constructed house consciously recreates the historic feeling of a classic Georgian home to provide a nurturing environment for a family with four children. It was carefully sited on its corner lot to optimize the footprint available for construction. The rigorous seismic design requirements of the location had to be addressed creatively in order to preserve the classical statement desired by the clients. Early in the design process the preservation of several large and beautiful live oak trees on the site was deemed a high

priority. To further enhance the beauty of the site, the garage is located below grade.

For the stone façade Eric Smith and the owners selected aged-faced granite cut from the abandoned fissures of a Connecticut quarry. These stones have a rare patina from exposure to the elements over many years, providing this new home with a sense of history. The variegated slate roof has a low slope to accommodate generous interior ceiling heights and tall windows.

An H-shaped plan provides most rooms with natural light from two or more aspects, and the classical organization of the interior spaces provides clarity through axial views and enfilades. Eric Smith designed the custom millwork, cabinetry, and plaster moldings. The kitchen was designed using Georgian

Gothick-inspired detailing, with a bronze and glass conservatory functioning as breakfast area and informal dining room. French doors and triple-hung windows with pocketed screens and shades open onto the gardens, which are formally planted close to the house and pool while in the background contrast is provided by a path that meanders through the perimeter trees and woodland plantings.

All images are used by permission of Eric J. Smith Architect.

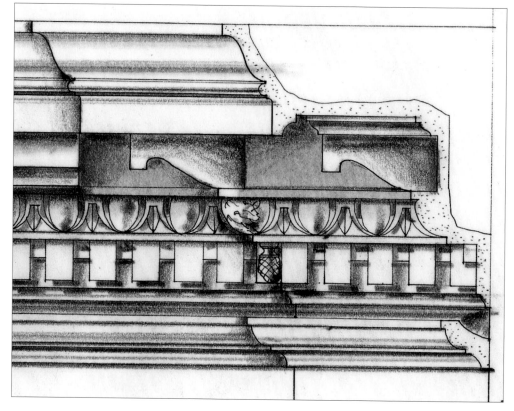

Portuondo Perotti Architects, Inc.

Miami, Florida

VILLA LAS BRISAS
Coral Gables, Florida

PROJECT TEAM:
Rafael Portuondo, *Principal and Lead Designer;*
Jose L. Gonzalez Perotti, *Principal and Architect;*
Andrea Bustamante, *Project Manager*

A client with a young family commissioned this villa for an extraordinary five-and-a-half-acre site situated on a promontory projecting into the Bay of Biscayne in the Gables Estates neighborhood of Coral Gables. The H-shaped parti takes maximum advantage of the available views over water on three sides of the site while at the same time enabling the clear separation of leisure activities such as swimming, tennis, and a putting green. Cars are handled with particular care through the creation of a deep U-shaped entrance forecourt framed by wings which, on a lower level, accommodate garages accessible from separate parking and service courts. The serious Cinquecento classicism of this arrival sequence gives way on the ocean front to a much more playful interpretation of the tradition: here a serliana arch in the upper loggia breaks through into a broad gable, which is framed by a deeply overhanging, polychromatic Tuscan cornice.

All images are used by permission of Portuondo Perotti Architects, Inc. Photography by Carlos Domenech and Katherine Pasternack.

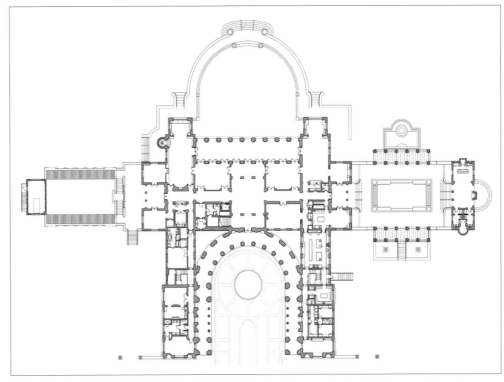

John Milner Architects, Inc.

Chadds Ford, Pennsylvania

A New Residence
Princeton, New Jersey

Project Team:
John D. Milner FAIA, *Principal-in-Charge*; Edward P. Wheeler AIA, *Project Architect*

The clients for this new residence near Princeton, New Jersey, were both raised in Federal Revival houses and wished to create a home with similar qualities that would also serve the practical needs of a young and active family. The result is a "relaxed" classicism, which features vernacular materials merged with traditional elements and detailing. The cut stone trim is variegated Ohio sandstone, set in a local-fieldstone wall, and the roof is a blue-grey Vermont slate. The home was sited with great care so as to respect the natural topography and to preserve the wooded nature of the large site. Dr. Barbara Paca prepared the comprehensive landscape design. Within the house, the enfilade is terminated to the south by a two-story library featuring a tall bow window, a mezzanine gallery with a wrought iron railing, and custom shelving for 10,000 volumes made from quarter-sawn white oak. An arcaded "thinking porch" with a fireplace with a carved sandstone mantelshelf opens from the library. The interior designer was Greg Jordan and the contractor was E. Allen Reeves, Inc.

All images are used by permission of John Milner Architects, Inc. Photographs by Matt Wargo.

Another Rome

THE ARCHITECTURE AND URBANISM OF ARMANDO BRASINI

By Steven W. Semes

At this point in time the comprehensive history of classical architecture in the twentieth century is yet to be written, and important designers languish in obscurity awaiting rediscovery. A notable tendency in the conventional historiography of modern architecture has been to disregard or suppress the work of architects who fell outside the narrow boundaries of what was acceptable stylistically or politically by postwar historians and critics.[1] This is particularly the case in those countries, like Italy, that suffered under varieties of fascism in the inter-war period. Only since the 1990s, and more so in recent years, has a younger generation of Italian scholars decisively broken with the postwar *damnatio memoriae* against the classical architects and traditional urbanists of the inter-war period and begun resurrecting the principal figures.[2]

Perhaps the most deserving beneficiary of this revisionist scholarship is the brilliant classical architect Armando Brasini (1879-1968), who, after nearly half a century of critical disregard, is the subject of newly sympathetic study by Italian scholars.[3] The aim of this essay is to present some of the fruits of this research, in particular, a review of four seminal built projects in Rome that reveal Brasini's approaches to formal language, construction materials and techniques, and the historic contexts in which he built. Many of his large-scale urban design proposals for the Eternal City raise challenging questions about urban theory and the conservation of historic centers. Brasini's work offers an essential example of visionary, dynamic, and highly inventive modern classical architecture that merits study alongside the work of his better-known contemporaries Edwin Lutyens and Bernard Maybeck, but also provides cautionary lessons for modern urbanism.

EARLY LIFE AND WORK

Like Lutyens and Maybeck, Brasini was an astonishingly talented designer from a modest background who seemed to emerge as a fully-formed artist with little or no formal education in architecture. Born Armando Stefano Ludovico Brasini in Rome on September 21, 1879, one of nine children of a tailor, Brasini's early schooling was limited to the elementary grades. His talent was recognized early and he was sent to the Istituto di Belle Arti, but he stayed only one year because of his "natural impetuousness."[4] He began his career as a painter, decorative plasterer, stone-carver, and sculptor, and by his late teens he had earned a reputation as a designer of ornament. Among other projects, he designed side chapels and a large sunburst frame for the icon over the main altar at the church of S. Maria dei Miracoli in Piazza del Popolo and the public reception rooms of the Hotel Excelsior on Via Veneto.

Brasini soon found his way into architectural practice, where his visual imagination led to strikingly innovative classical designs. A youthful example is his entrance gate for the Rome zoo, won in a competition of 1909, which features sculpted elephant heads as keystones, trunks probing the archivolts below [FIGURE 2]. Three years later, another competition entry for rebuilding the north end of Piazza Navona in a conforming baroque style, designed in a unique partnership with Marcello Piacentini, received first prize but was never implemented [FIGURE 3].[5] Brasini's seemingly innate and intuitive

Opposite: Armando Brasini, INAIL Building (Cassa Nazionale Assicurazioni Infortuni di Lavoro), via IV novembre, Rome, 1926-32. Photograph by Steven Semes.

Figure 1 (above): Armando Brasini, detail of self portrait, from Luca Brasini, *L'opera architettonica e urbanistica di Armando Brasini* (Rome: [s.n.], 1979).

Figure 2 (above): Armando Brasini, monumental entrance to the Giardino Zoologico, Rome, 1909. Photograph by Massimiliano Di Giovanni (Courtesy of the Archivio Bioparco, *www.bioparco.it*)

Figure 3 (left): Armando Brasini and Marcello Piacentini, competition design for rebuilding the northern end of the Piazza Navona, Rome, 1912. View of plaster model, from Paolo Orano, *L'urbe massima: l'architettura e la decorazione di Armando Brasini* (Rome: A. F. Formiggini, 1917).

Figure 4 (page 46): Armando Brasini, INAIL Building (Cassa Nazionale Assicurazioni Infortuni di Lavoro), via IV novembre, Rome, 1926-32. Photograph by Steven Semes.

Figure 5 (page 47): Armando Brasini, perspective view of the INAIL Building, Rome, from Luca Brasini, *L'opera architettonica e urbanistica di Armando Brasini* (Rome: [s.n.], 1979).

understanding of the Roman Baroque led to the 1917 commission to restore and remodel Giacomo della Porta's late sixteenth-century Palazzo Chigi as a government ministry. Throughout his career, perhaps because of his early training as a *stuccatore*, he continued to design using plaster models as well as drawing to explore his architectural ideas. This may explain why Brasini's work retains a three-dimensional dynamism, a sculptural vitality difficult to grasp in orthographic representations. His formative experience in the building crafts led him to a mastery of materials and detailing that gives a robust artisanal quality to even his most carefully composed conceptions.

For Brasini, as for many of his contemporaries, restoration work and the design of new buildings were aspects of a single discipline rooted in the tradition shared by both the historic and the contemporary architect. There was no sense of obligation to "differentiate" the new work from the old. Historical monuments existed not only to be conserved, but also to be extended by new contributions that promised relevance in the future without fundamentally altering their character. This sense of continuity is apparent throughout Brasini's architectural projects, as attested by his proposals to complete the dome of Sant'Ignazio, remodel the Palazzo Venezia, complete the Vittorio Emanuele II Monument, and design the adjacent Museo del Risorgimento.

MATURE ARCHITECTURAL WORK: INAIL BUILDING

From the riches of his long and varied career, a brief examination of four of Brasini's best known executed buildings in Rome reveals the character of his approach and taste. The Casa Nazionale Infortuni from 1926-32 emerges as a conspicuous landmark at the head of Via IV Novembre, visible from Piazza Venezia, the symbolic central crossroads of modern Rome [FIGURE 4]. A work of which Lutyens would surely have been proud, the structure, now known as the INAIL building, is a key work of the architect's maturity. The history of the project is as complex as the difficulties imposed by its irregular and topographically challenging site, with debates about the building's size and style compounded by lawsuits filed by neighboring property owners, relentless satires in the press, Senate hearings, and, finally, personal intervention by Mussolini himself. The prominent site, formerly that of the Teatro Drammatico Nazionale designed by Francesco Azzuri (1884), demanded a building of monumental character and its financing a maximum return.[6]

Brasini was joined on the project by the respected engineer Guido Zevi, whose son, the critic Bruno Zevi, would later lead the postwar campaign against his father's former collaborator.[7] The elder Zevi, responsible for technical direction, permitting, and construction administration, assured that the building would have every technological advantage, while Brasini's artistic direction was aimed at providing a suitably decorous and "Roman" landmark. Initially designed as a speculative venture by the public utility EGR, the project was acquired by the Cassa Nazionale Infortuni (now known as INAIL) as headquarters for the agency responsible for administering disability insurance for industrial workers. Consequently, the building's character was dictated more by urban design considerations than by a specific program or user.[8]

Each of the elevations received a different treatment in response to diverse conditions, but from the start the main consideration was to provide a "scenic backdrop" to the view from the Piazza Venezia. The principal (west) elevation is composed of two distinct but coordinated volumes, each addressing one of two scales. The tall and strongly modeled brick mass of the upper part addresses the distant view, presenting a two-bay (and therefore "center-occupied"), double-height loggia as a large-scale gesture that also masks the repetitive windows typical of office buildings. The lower volume steps forward as an *avant-corps* responding to the closer view while providing a graceful connection to the adjacent Villa Colonna, the *ninfeo* of which is echoed in Brasini's convex façade. The axis of the lower volume is shifted from that of the upper in recognition of the narrow frontage and the centerline of the street leading towards it. The arched main entrance is framed by Doric columns projecting from the dour rusticated façade in travertine, while the brick and stone upper volume is notable for its chiaroscuro effects and Michelangelesque detailing. Brasini's composition is essentially scenographic: There is an apparent lack of unity between the two parts in orthographic elevation, but the work appears unified when viewed in situ due to the constrained urban setting. The architect's perspective drawing illustrates how the complex massing steps its way up the hillside from the single-story wing adjacent to the Villa Colonna to the crowning belvedere above [FIGURE 5].[9] In both plan and elevation, local symmetries are carefully maintained within an overall asymmetrical composition, giving the complex a vitality and dynamism characteristic of all of Brasini's work.[10]

The interior, mostly given to office space, includes a dramatic promenade from the entrance *androne* to the internal courtyard, up the grand stair (first a straight flight and then a fantastic elliptical one), to a grand reception room at the *piano nobile* giving onto the terrace on top of the lower volume, from which one may look back toward the Piazza Venezia, where the sequence began conceptually.[11]

Although the controversies surrounding the project were more about conflicting private interests than design or style, they nonetheless cast a shadow over Brasini's career and his reputation suffered after the building's completion in 1932. The previous year, Pier Maria Bardi, a propagandist for the Rationalist MIAR group, included the INAIL building at the center of his "Tavola degli Orrori" (Panel of Horrors), an accusatory collage created for the Second Exposition of Rationalist Architecture, in which recent traditional architecture in Rome was ridiculed.[12] The previous year, Brasini had been the only Italian entrant in the competition for the Palace of the Soviets in Moscow, for which he received a mention, but his grandiloquent scheme celebrating Lenin apparently angered Il Duce.[13] About this time, writing directly to Mussolini, Brasini complained of being passed over for the most important state commissions; in the succeeding years before the Second World War brought all building activity to a halt, he received the Museo del Risorgimento, the Naples home of the Istituto Fascista della Previdenza Sociale (Fascist Institute of Social Services, later home of the Banca Nazionale del Lavoro), the Ponte Flaminio (at his own initiative and without fee), and the Agriculture and Forestry Building at EUR (left incomplete during the war and demolished afterward).

These are but a handful of commissions, however, considering the massive projects then underway in Rome and the renown that Brasini had enjoyed throughout the preceding decade.[14] The INAIL Building, therefore, can be regarded as the high point of Brasini's state commissions in the capital and a pivotal one in his own career trajectory.

COMPLEX OF THE BUON PASTORE

Considered the architect's masterpiece, the Convent of the Buon Pastore is a prominent landmark in the western *periferia* of Rome [FIGURES 6, 7, 8, AND 9]. Originally designed for a religious institution in 1929 and completed in 1943, it was later converted into a hospital and currently houses two high schools. Such adaptability to varied functions is especially notable given the work's highly idiosyncratic character. That same adaptability, however, also contributed to the building's unfortunate physical changes later and the removal of important decorative elements. Today, much of it is in need of restoration.

Surrounded by open countryside when completed, the complex retains the appearance of a little *"cittadella,"* or walled town rather than a building. Indeed, in this work Brasini seems to have "unfolded a personal catalogue of classical architecture."[15] Accordingly, the exterior has an austere and defensive character, but the central chapel—with a tall dome that would have delighted Borromini—faces a T-shaped courtyard surrounded by extraordinarily airy and delicate arcades. Although the plan composition is as disciplined and symmetrical as any Beaux-Arts exercise, the three-dimensional experience opens up a sequence of picturesque vistas, creating a dreamlike and unexpected piling-up of idiosyncratic structural and decorative elements at different scales. These nevertheless compose a satisfyingly complex whole, unified by the symmetries of the plan and revealing striking visual relationships, such as the perfectly framed view of the top of the dome captured for the approaching visitor by the central upper opening of the entrance façade. As in the INAIL building, Brasini observes Vitruvian decorum, reserving for entrances and public spaces the most intense articulation of parts and decorative detail, and assigning a more modest expression to less exalted areas. Despite occasionally jarring juxtapositions, the massive masonry walls, monumental Orders on pedestals, graceful arcades, and figural sculptures are carefully proportioned and scaled, thoughtfully coded to visually guide the visitor through the complex.

It was this multifarious but internally coherent character, with its hybrid of gothic and baroque tendencies, that attracted the attention of Robert Venturi, who in 1966 described the work as "an orgy of inflections of enormous scope…[that] astonishingly composes a multitude of diverse parts into a difficult whole. At all levels of scale it is an example of inflections within inflections successively directed toward different centers…like the unraveling of a symphony."[16] Characteristically, Venturi emphasized the asymmetries and inflections while we can suppose that the rigorously unified whole was more important to the architect. Perhaps more important still was Brasini's deep meditation on the building culture of Rome and its particular *genius loci*. As noted by Franco Borsi, "Rome is made of walls, of walls often paradoxical… massive, undulating, carved, shaped by the architect as a sculptural

material. And in the walls lies the mystery of architecture. All this in Brasini is not rhetoric, it is instinct."[17]

BASILICA OF THE SACRO CUORE IMMACOLATO DI MARIA

Design work for the Basilica of the Immaculate Heart of Mary in the Parioli neighborhood began in 1923 with construction continuing into the 1950s. The church, however, remains incomplete. The plan is geometrically disciplined—a Greek Cross inscribed in a circle with four chapels arrayed on the diagonals [FIGURE 10]—and Brasini described it as "a form both new and yet very classical . . . the setting of a sumptuous cross in a halo and a sunburst."[18] Although it is tempting to see the church as an exercise in neo-baroque, the designer himself likened his plan to the centralized churches of Sangallo and Michelangelo and admitted a desire to reflect "Vitruvius more than Bernini."[19] Brasini's ink drawings of his first, more ambitious scheme resembles nothing so much as Piranesian views of ancient Roman baths. The exterior as built, predominantly of brick with a bold Doric Order and punctuating elements in travertine, powerfully suggests a Roman ruin—the great buttresses holding up the Colosseum come to mind—or perhaps a late Renaissance church undergoing a slow-motion explosion pressing its massive columns, entablatures, and pediments outward with tremendous force [FIGURE 11]. The structure we see appears disproportionately massive because it was intended as the base of an unexecuted drum and dome rivaling Saint Peter's in scale. These would have held the composition together with an unqualified vertical emphasis, as we can see in his drawings and plaster model [FIGURE 12].

The spacious interior, inspired again by Roman bath complexes but more sober in decoration, reveals unexpected perspectives in the interstices between the orthogonal nave and the circular ambulatory; but here we feel even more keenly the absence of the visual climax and abundant light that would have been provided by the missing drum and dome. Except for the stately Corinthian order, the intended decorative scheme remains unexecuted in the nave but we can get some idea of the architect's original intentions in the two chapels he completed [FIGURE 13]. Even in its truncated state, and bereft of its intended decorative sculpture, the Basilica has a forceful, expressive character typical of Brasini's mature work. Several years before beginning work on Sacro Cuore, Brasini designed a dome for the seventeenth-century Baroque church of Sant'Ignazio, similarly lacking its intended culminating feature. Brasini's large plaster model for the Sant'Ignazio dome gives us an indication of what the dome of the Parioli church might have been like [FIGURE 14].[20]

To Venturi the absence of the dome is a "circumstance [that] diminishes the historical literalism of the architecture and establishes the building, in my opinion, as a grand and fortuitous fragment—as an unfinished symphony." Venturi notes that the church's incompleteness "makes the rhetoric of the now functionless buttresses more poignant and eloquent."[21] Venturi's rather romantic interpretation of the project as built irritated Brasini's son Luca, who considered this reading a misunderstanding of the architect's intentions.[22] While the nineteenth-century Romantics as well as modernists like Venturi or Louis Kahn

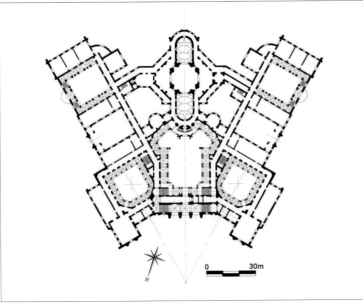

Figure 6 (top left): Armando Brasini, Complesso del Buon Pastore, Rome, 1929-43. Photograph by Steven Semes.

Figure 7 (left): Armando Brasini, Complesso del Buon Pastore, Rome. Ground floor plan, drawn by Assen Assenov.

Figure 8 (top right): Armando Brasini, Complesso del Buon Pastore, Rome. Main courtyard. Photograph by Steven Semes.

Figure 9 (above): Armando Brasini, Complesso del Buon Pastore, Rome. Dome of chapel.

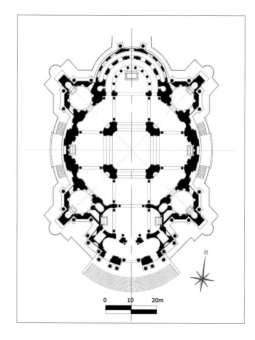

often found poetic inspiration in the ruined state of ancient Rome, for Brasini the value of the ruins lay precisely in the opportunity to learn from them and reconstruct them, whether graphically or physically.[23]

VITTORIO EMANUELE II MONUMENT
AND THE MUSEUM OF THE RISORGIMENTO

The Vittorio Emanuele II Monument, known as the Vittoriano, is both the most conspicuous landmark of modern Rome and the most important national patriotic site in the capital city. Designed by Giuseppe Sacconi in 1882, its strict Imperial Roman style and gleaming white marble intentionally distinguished it from the Baroque Rome of the popes, which the new Italian state was then transforming into the capital of a secular nation [FIGURE 15]. Controversial from its inception, there are many things about the structure that continue to rankle, its isolation from the city compounded by the later demolition of its surrounding buildings by Mussolini. And yet there is no denying the monumental grandeur of Sacconi's design, its masterful management of multiple scale levels from the urban to the ornamental, its elegant classical detail, and its superbly integrated sculptural elements.

In 1924 Brasini was named artistic director of the Monument and oversaw its completion in 1933, having designed the monument's principal interiors, including the tomb of the Unknown Soldier and the Hall of the Flags, and adding the Museum of the Risorgimento on the east side [FIGURE 16]. Brasini's long association with the Vittoriano is undoubtedly a key source of his sense of monumental character, orthodox classical grammar, and inventive composition. It is also likely that it inspired his urban visions of monumental buildings conceived as freestanding sculptures in vast open spaces, a tendency contrary to the meticulously harmonious insertion of his own additions to the site.[24]

Brasini himself regarded his work on the Museum as the most valid of his career.[25] It was also perhaps the most technically demanding: a new structure constrained by the Vittoriano on one side; on the other, the ruins of the Augustan wall, the ancient Arx, and the cliff-face of the Capitol hill with Vignola's portico directly above. He used the local palette of brick, travertine, and *peperino* to harmonize with the Capitoline buildings and gave the dignified but deferential façade the character of a massive retaining wall, with buttresses, battered walls, and layered arches framing the entrance. The new construction is so thoroughly woven into its complex setting that, as the architect later remarked, it is better grasped by a sequence of close-up views than a perspective of the ensemble.[26] Brasini's intervention is a reweaving of disparate elements spanning twenty centuries and, while close observation allows us to distinguish his work from pre-existing structures, there is no attempt at contrast or introduction of materials or motifs alien to the site. Consequently, the Museum serves as a model for an intervention both "differentiated" and "compatible" with respect to its historic setting (with the balance decisively tipped toward the latter).[27]

GENERAL OBSERVATIONS

This brief review of four of Brasini's built projects in Rome allows us to identify the extent of his devotion to the classical tradition as well as his innovations within it. In the first instance, his embrace of the classical was active and transformative, a vital re-reading of the tradition that he saw as ongoing and alive. His innovations typically present in the overall composition rather than the details. There is little in his decorative or ornamental language that would puzzle Hadrian or Borromini, but a penchant for fantasy characterizes his conception of the building as a whole and the disposition of its major parts. For example, his classical Orders, used with decorous restraint and appearing in full only at the most important moments, are generally canonical in proportion and ornament; but the disparate characterization of the upper and lower volumes of the INAIL building, the courtyard and chapel dome at Buon Pastore, and the layered entrance porch of Sacro Cuore are prime examples of his inventiveness at a larger scale.

In the evolution of these projects we also see a process of formal editing, a progressive simplification of the expressive language in which the architect's focus appears to shift from ornamental detail to the expressive power of unadorned masses. Brasini shares this tendency with numerous contemporaries who, throughout the inter-war period, tended progressively to emphasize mass, silhouette, and medium-scale articulation over smaller-scaled embellishment.[28] The motives for this appear to be an impulse to find greater expressiveness in abstract form, an interest in revealing the material facts of construction in the face of declining decorative

Figure 10 (opposite, top left): Armando Brasini, Basilica del Sacro Cuore Immacolato di Maria, Rome, 1923-1955. Plan, drawn by Assen Assenov.

Figure 11 (opposite, bottom): Armando Brasini, Basilica del Santo Cuore Immacolato di Maria, Rome, 1923-55. Photograph by Steven Semes.

Figure 12 (opposite, top middle): Armando Brasini, Basilica del Santo Cuore Immacolato di Maria, Rome, 1923-55. Architect's model showing dome, from Luca Brasini, *L'opera architettonica e urbanistica di Armando Brasini* (Rome: [s.n.], 1979).

Figure 13 (opposite, top right): Armando Brasini, Basilica del Santo Cuore Immacolato di Maria, Rome, 1923-55. Photograph by Steven Semes.

Figure 14 (above): Armando Brasini, Model of Proposed Dome for Sant'Ignazio, Rome. Photograph by Mattes.

craftsmanship, and the need to adapt traditional forms and typologies to new uses.[29] The progressively austere language of detail is compensated for by greater freedom of composition: Brasini's designs are typically dynamic, sometimes asymmetrical, and modeled for maximum effect in perspectival views, as at the INAIL building. Throughout his career, a "philologically incorrect" combination of classical types and figures flouts academic correctness in favor of a stylistic "contamination" that draws on motifs from a variety of sources, including the modern—albeit the "other modern" that mixed traditional and new forms rather than the formal purism of the modernist avant-garde—though Brasini was not immune to influence even from the rival Rationalists.[30]

Brasini's work displays a consistent structural realism inseparable from the formal composition: the battered walls, buttresses, arches, and other elements all play their respective roles in ways that are simultaneously tectonic and expressive. This attention to the poetics of construction also contributed to the process of simplification as the inevitable regularity of load-bearing masonry systems imposed its own satisfying logic in the same way it had for the ancients.[31] Finally, Brasini took seriously his obligation to fulfill a building task that, in most cases, was unmistakably modern, such as the office building or museum. Clients too exerted pressure, subtle or otherwise, to simplify and economize the designs. Brasini seems to have been mostly accommodating, as in his "painful" reduction of his first design for Sacro Cuore and the many revisions to his several schemes for the Ponte Flaminio.[32]

Figure 16 (above): Armando Brasini, Museo del Risorgimento, Rome, 1924-33. Photograph by Steven Semes.

Figure 17 (opposite): Armando Brasini, Aerial view of proposed *spina nuova,* Vatican City, 1917, from Paolo Orano, *L'urbe massima: l'architettura e la decorazione di Armando Brasini* (Rome: A. F. Formiggini, 1917).

STUDIES IN URBANISM: "L'URBE MASSIMA"

Brasini pursued his interest in urbanism throughout his career. By 1917, he had published a folio of drawings and photographs of plaster models entitled *L'urbe Massima* containing designs for urban interventions of extraordinary audacity and imagination.[33] The visionary images of the folio immediately recall the fantasies of Piranesi and the "revolutionary" architecture of the French designers Claude-Nicolas Ledoux and Etienne-Louis Boullée.[34] Brasini shares with them a rhetorical grandiloquence, a preference for grand gestures at a colossal scale, and a general lack of interest in the exigencies of contemporary urban life. Some of his large-scale proposals also presuppose an urbanism based on object-buildings isolated in enormous open spaces, in contrast to the contextual sensitivity of his realized architectural projects. It is worthwhile to look more closely at two of these youthful urban proposals.

Ever since Bernini completed the Piazza San Pietro, numerous proposals have been offered to replace the *spina* of the medieval *borghi* with an axial approach connecting the piazza with Castel Sant'Angelo and the Tiber, including one by Bernini himself.[35] All such schemes eliminated the surprise of suddenly emerging into the great square from the narrow medieval streets and instead opened an axial vista from the basilica to the river. This arrangement was realized by Marcello Piacentini's Via della Conciliazione, planned in 1936 and completed in 1950, resulting in an uninterrupted, and therefore telescoped view of the basilica from the Tiber. Instead, Brasini blocks the axis by a 250 meter-long *nuova spina*—a covered passage based on Bernini's colonnades [FIGURE 17]. The pedestrian would gain a view of the square only upon arrival at the monumental loggia at the west end; from there, as in Bernini's own scheme for a freestanding loggia in this location, the *terza braccia*, the observer would have an ideally composed view of the piazza and Basilica. Brasini's renderings reveal a Baroque vision rivaling Bernini's own and the scheme, conceived as a devotional pilgrimage route rather than a grand venue for military parades, is reminiscent of Carlo Francesco Dotti's arcades leading to the Sanctuary of the Madonna of Saint Luke in Bologna [FIGURE 18].[36] The proposal was also one that could be built within the void left by Piacentini's intervention, but even decades later Brasini was unable to interest either the state or the Vatican in his proposal.[37]

He had better success with his proposal for a monumental double bridge to carry the Via Flaminia across the Tiber, a project shown in astonishing perspective views featuring great cascades that spill from mid-span and a central fountain [FIGURE 19]. The actual project was finally granted to him in 1930, after strenuous lobbying and offering to donate his fees. Brasini's revised design was officially accepted in 1938: a single span without the waterworks but including a monumental triumphal arch supporting a colossal statue of Mussolini. After the war, with the bridge already under construction, the commemorative elements were eliminated and a much-simplified design was completed in 1951, still affording a fitting entrance to the city [FIGURE 20].[38]

PLAN FOR THE CAMPO MARZIO

Brasini began to develop proposals for the Campo Marzio (the largely medieval and Renaissance quarter of Rome in the bend of the Tiber

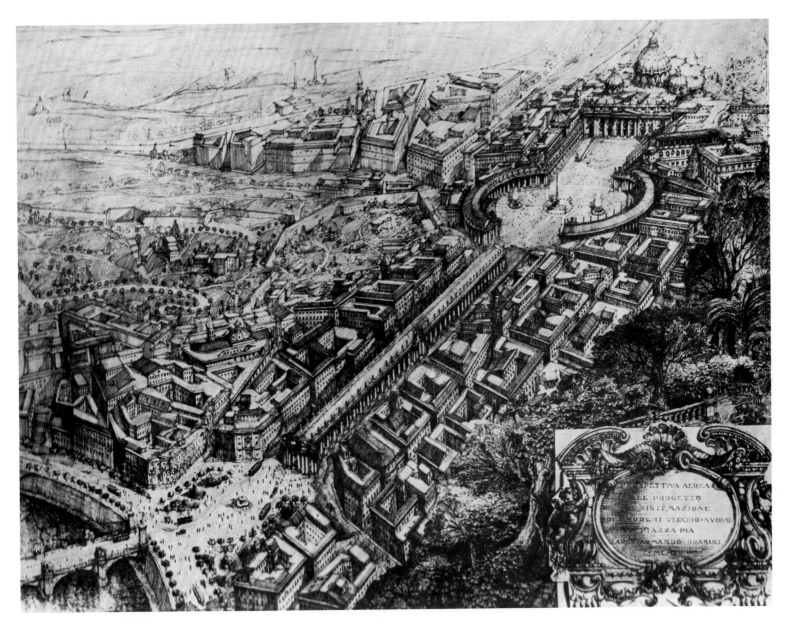

west of the Via del Corso) in 1918, and he compiled and published these in 1927 [FIGURE 21].[39] His presentation further developed some of the themes and sites explored in the 1917 folio, but now at an enlarged scale encompassing the entire historic center and revealing "a new Rome whose urban ensemble would seem modern and archeological at the same time."[40] The centerpiece of the plan was a broad new thoroughfare winding its way through the center, the Via Imperiale, linking the Ponte Flaminio in the north to the Via Appia in the south and providing a "grandiose and monumental frame" for the principal sites of the ancient Imperial and Baroque city. The climax of the new itinerary was to be the Foro Mussolini, an immense open space extending from the Piazza Colonna through the Piazza di Montecitorio to the Senate and then south to the Pantheon.[41]

Brasini's plan would have required demolition of historic fabric on a then-unprecedented scale. Certainly, preservation in the modern sense was entirely absent from Brasini's thinking, and he considered the loss of post-antique urban fabric a reasonable price to pay for the exhumation of buried antiquities or the creation of more dramatic settings for the most important post-antique monuments.[42] For example, he proposed the demolition of the entire neighborhood between Sant'Andrea della Valle and the Largo Argentina to allow excavation of the Portico and Theater of Pompey. He would remove and reconstruct on another site Filippo Raguzzini's complex on the Piazza Sant'Ignazio—which he dismissively described as a *scenetta goldoniana* (a quaint rococo stage-set)— in order to provide a more dramatic vista of the Baroque church façade that looms over them. The remains of the Temple of Hadrian, so skillfully woven into the Dogana di Terra by Carlo and Francesco Fontana (1691-1700) and remodeled for the Borsa in 1874 by Virginio Vespignani, were to be isolated and set up as a freestanding ruin in the vastness of the new Foro Mussolini [FIGURE 22]. At strategic points in this altered fabric he proposed grandiose new construction—including a "basilica Mussoliniana," a lavish new market and commercial center, and a new palace for the Senate—on a scale that perhaps would have made even Hadrian blush.

Even though the proposed clearance understandably provoked intense criticism and accusations of "megalomania"[43], individual set pieces in his plan merit study as hypothetical *esquisses*. Particularly striking is the use of monumental stairs and fountains to unify the piazzas and mediate between grade levels in front of the Pantheon and the Palazzo del Montecitorio. Also intriguing are his proposals to lower the Via dei Fori Imperiali and the streets around the Mausoleum of Augustus to the grade of the ancient Roman city, providing access to the ancient remains and allowing their integration into the fabric of the modern city.[44]

Curiously, his Campo Marzio scheme reflects the geometrical irregularities of the Roman Forum rather than the formal order and figural space of the Imperial Forums, and the immense open space shown in front of the Pantheon bears no resemblance to the rectangular and more appropriately-scaled colonnaded forecourt, which existed there in antiquity.[45] While the urbanism of the Baroque is recalled in the long vistas linking one monument to another and in the design of the individual set pieces, largely absent from Brasini's presentation is the Baroque concept of the city as a sequence of formally composed, geometrically ordered outdoor rooms enclosed by continuous façades. Similarly, the incremental approach of Baroque interventions reflecting necessary compromises among the "enmities and alliances" of patrons is far removed from Brasini's all-but-*tabula-rasa* approach.[46]

Perhaps most striking to the contemporary reader is the cinematic character of his written description, as if he were presenting a screenplay for an epic film set in an imagined Rome of the Emperors. He wrote:

> *Crossing the Corso Vittorio Emanuele, parallel with the side of the Palazzo Altieri and the Church of the Gesù, the Via Imperiale would be on axis with the Theater of Marcellus, framed on the right by the grandiose pile of the Palazzo Caetani and on the left by the eighteenth-century Palazzo Cenci Bolognetti by Ferdinando Fuga. Bending to the east, on the right one sees the harmonious and majestic backdrop of the Campidoglio and ahead, on axis, the impressive mass of the Vittoriano. From this point one enjoys an architectural panorama of striking beauty the principal elements of which are the Vittoriano—with the Capitoline Arx in its triumphal and Roman setting—the Church of Ara Coeli, the Palazzo di Venezia, the Column and Markets of Trajan, and the Churches of Santa Maria Loreto and Santissimo Nome di Maria. Continuing below the Capitoline Arx, the Via Imperiale is flanked on the left by the Forums of Trajan, Augustus, Caesar, and Nerva and the Forum of Peace in all their superb Roman grandeur, and on the right by the Roman Forum and the glory of the Palatine with all its monuments. One then descends to the Colosseo and from there the broad Via di San Giovanni, appropriately widened, reaches the Piazza di San Giovanni in Laterano and, through the Porta Asinaria, flows into the Via Appia.*[47]

Figure 15 (top): Giuseppe Sacconi, Vittorio Emanuele II Monument, Rome, 1882. Photograph by Dan Kamminga.

Figure 18 (center): C. F. Dotti, Madonna di San Luca, Bologna, 1723. Photograph by Paige Miller.

Figure 19 (bottom): Armando Brasini, Perspective view of proposed new Ponte Flaminio, Rome, 1917, from Paolo Orano, *L'urbe massima: l'architettura e la decorazione di Armando Brasini* (Rome: A. F. Formiggini, 1917).

Figure 20 (opposite): Armando Brasini, Ponte Flaminio, Rome. Photograph by Pierreci.

The cinematic connection was no accident. Brasini had designed the sets for the Italian films *Theodora* (1919) and *Quo Vadis?* (1923), and his connection with the production company of the latter was a key factor in obtaining the commission for the INAIL project. For *Quo Vadis?* the interior sets were constructed to Brasini's designs and the exterior locations featured the buildings erected by Brasini for an exposition of Roman art and architecture in the park of the Villa Borghese the same year—an elaborate, if temporary, Roman "city" complete with houses, streets, porticoes, *piazze*, triumphal arches, and an imperial palace with a monumental fountain fed by the waters of the lagoon.[48] The Campo Marzio plan seems a direct extension of that scenographic exercise into the real city, at a vast scale and with all the contradictions doing so implies.[49]

EVALUATING BRASINI'S URBAN PROPOSALS

Gigantism and monumentality were not unique to Brasini's urban visions; indeed, they share aspects of both academic and modernist approaches common at the time. Designs for enormous buildings isolated in huge open spaces were produced by many architects trained at the École des Beaux-Arts in Paris during the Third Empire, or elsewhere under Parisian influence including such American examples as the 1909 Plan for Chicago by Daniel Burnham.[50] In Rome, Mussolini's clearance operations around the Capitoline Hill and between the Vittoriano and Piazza Venezia represent a Roman application of this "academic" urbanism.[51] The modernists, too, employed a visual rhetoric of gigantic masses isolated in open space, as in the industrial-inspired fantasies of Antonio Sant'Elia or the dark skyscraper visions of Hugh Ferriss.[52] A similar intent to isolate monuments prompted the Rationalists' entries to the 1934 competition for the Palazzo Littorio, the Fascist party headquarters, on the newly opened Via dell'Impero immediately opposite the Colosseum, and the 1938 competition for a Piazza Imperiale at EUR, to cite but two examples.[53]

In contrast to both the academic and modernist approaches is the traditionalist urbanism of Camillo Sitte, represented in Italy by the *ambientismo* of Gustavo Giovannoni.[54] In this view, individual buildings draw their significance from their relations to other buildings and historic monuments are valued in part for being embedded in a fabric of more modest "minor architecture." The pragmatic routing of the Corso Vittorio Emanuele II or the Corso del Rinascimento, avoiding straight-line boulevards slashing through the old fabric and maximizing the retention of historic structures, reflects Giovannoni's theory of *diradamento* ("thinning" or "pruning") in contrast to Hausmannesque *sventramenti* ("gutting"). The parallel between this latter approach and Brasini's plan prompted much of the criticism directed against it. Giovannoni, who referred to the Campo Marzio scheme as a "catastrophe," was also particularly vocal in opposing the destruction of the *spina* of the Vatican *borghi*, shown in Brasini's plan and later carried out by Piacentini.[55] In 1930, Ugo Ojetti, the editor of *Dedalo* and an advocate for the traditionalists' viewpoint, saw the problem with Brasini's urban vision as a matter of scale: "If he will permit me, the problem is in (Brasini's) persuasion that grandeur is synonymous with vastness, and that vastness is synonymous with Roman. Vast indeed was the Roman Empire, but not the dimensions of all the streets and *piazze* of Rome."[56]

Brasini's urban proposals indicate—albeit in an extreme form—the freedom with which an architect might propose radical change at a time when contemporary architectural culture was viewed by the public as capable or likely to produce new buildings equal or superior in quality to those to be removed.[57] But this does not explain the contrast between the sensitivity to scale and context with which Brasini inserted the INAIL Building or the Museum of the Risorgimento into their highly challenging sites and the cavalier attitude toward existing fabric shown in his Campo Marzio plans. Were the urban design proposals an attempted escape from the constraints of the hemmed-in contexts he found in many of his professional projects?

For his part, Mussolini proclaimed in a 1925 speech that the monuments of ancient Rome should "loom gigantic in their necessary solitude," and by 1928 began demolishing the Vatican's Via Alessandrina neighborhood and clearing the slopes of the Capitoline, destroying

thousands of structures and displacing tens of thousands of residents.[58] Brasini's role in the regime's urban clearance program is not evident, although his Campo Marzio plans seem largely to embody the Duce's vision. Brasini later seems to claim credit for Mussolini's policies and schemes, noting bitterly that components of his proposals were realized by other architects.[59] Further research may shed light on the scope of his official role, if any; what is clear now is that the two men "shared the dream of a new imperial Rome," though in Brasini's case it can be argued that he was motivated by "an innocent dream of grandeur" detached from any particular political program—or real-life consequences.[60]

ARCHITECTURE AND POLITICS

Brasini's urban design schemes clearly draw inspiration from the triumphalism of Imperial Rome and Bernini's work for Alexander VII, appealing to a generalized concept of Glory in the face of rising radical socialism and the modernist avant-garde in the years following World War I. In this context, Brasini's proposals appeared culturally reactionary and, not surprisingly, attracted the interest of the fascist dictatorship for its own propaganda purposes. But Mussolini's interest in classical design as a sign of continuity with the glories of Roman antiquity was qualified by an equal interest in the rival Rationalists, who passionately argued for an Italian version of international modernism as the true expression of the fascist spirit.[61] The Duce's apparent duplicity in these stylistic debates—appearing to support now one side, now the other—reflected his desire to balance the appeal to tradition with the imperatives of modern military-industrial development, something in which Brasini had little interest.[62]

Given the complexities and contradictions of the political and cultural climate during the decades of his most productive professional activity, and the complicated relationship between Brasini and the Duce, we must be cautious in identifying specific political content in his designs and avoid the use of the term "fascist" as a stylistic label rather than a purely political or chronological one.[63] Brasini's motivations were evidently more romantic than political, as reflected in his non-ideological willingness to dedicate his architectural extravaganzas in turn to the King of Italy and to the Pope, to Lenin and to Mussolini, without stylistic distinction. This apparent neutrality, whether due to opportunism or naiveté, was also exhibited by many of his professional colleagues, regardless of stylistic bent or political sympathies.[64] Ultimately, Brasini's designs seem "intended exclusively to exalt the idea of the monument itself,"[65] and perhaps given the "outside of time" character of much of his work, he also imagined the ambiguous content of his monuments as a way "to leave the building available for the expression of what it may yet become, projecting its possible future."[66]

CONCLUSION

Brasini's architecture reveals for us another Rome—one unexplored by tourists, still absent from the standard histories and guidebooks, and virtually unknown outside of Italy—a Rome in which, for a couple of decades between the wars, modernity and tradition contested with one another fruitfully, yielding work that we can consider "traditional" and

at the same time modern in its inventiveness and risk-taking. Now free to study this other Rome without prejudice, we can return Brasini's work to the historical mainstream, placing it within what is now recognized as the "other modern," an architecture freed from the narrow ideological focus and stylistic purity of the Modern Movement.[67] We can also now appreciate why post-war critics wanted Brasini to "disappear." His work resists dismissal as pastiche or kitsch, or the last vestiges of an exhausted style. His designs were not academic or antiquarian but robust, passionate, grand, imaginative, innovative, baroque, and often "over the top." In other words, they were Roman. He seemed to work in a realm outside of time, one in which all the great classical architecture of the past was still contemporary,[68] and stubbornly refused to conform to the grand narrative in which architectural production in the early twentieth century was judged important to the extent it prefigured or participated in the Modern Movement and its Italian variant, Rationalism. On the other hand, the current generation of classical architects should not approach Brasini's work uncritically: His work raises challenging questions about the limits of visual imagination in architecture, the architect's associations with political power, and the appropriate relationship of contemporary and pre-existing

construction in historic centers. Still, the explosive formal invention and technical mastery of Brasini's built works might yet serve as a catalyst for a reinvigorated and more expressive modern classical architecture—its composition and formal language fearless and adventurous once again.❧

Steven W. Semes is a Fellow Emeritus of the ICAA and is Associate Professor at the University of Notre Dame School of Architecture.

Figure 21 (opposite): Armando Brasini, Plan for the Campo Marzio, Rome, 1927. From catalog of the exhibition, "Armando Brasini: Roma Imperiale," Edmonton Gallery of Art, 1978, plate 10, used with permission of the Art Gallery of Alberta.

Figure 22 (above): Armando Brasini, Plan for the Campo Marzio, Rome, 1927. Detail of aerial view, showing Piazza Sant'Ignazio, lower left; expanded Piazza Colonna, lower right; and new square at the Pantheon, upper center. From the catalog of the exhibition, "Armando Brasini: Roma Imperiale," Edmonton Gallery of Art, 1977, plate 21, used with permission of the Art Gallery of Alberta.

NOTES

I would like to record my gratitude to the following: Professor Ettore Maria Mazzola of the University of Notre Dame Rome Studies Program for re-introducing me to Brasini's life and works, and Professor Lorenzo Bartolini Salimbeni of the Università di Pescara for his introduction to recent scholarship on the Italian architects of the "other modern." Donald Clinton and Karen Wilkin for sharing their knowledge of the subject of their 1978 exhibition and catalogue for the Edmonton Art Gallery. Professor Richard Piccolo for allowing his copy of the Paolo Orano folio to be reproduced for some of the illustrations for this article. Assen Assenov for making the valuable new plan drawings in addition to other technical assistance. The American Academy in Rome and Robert A. M. Stern Architects, New York, for access to their libraries, and to David Pearson in the office of the latter. Elisabetta Procida, Curator of the Brasini Archive, for her assistance in obtaining permission for the reproduction of drawings. Special thanks are due to Luisa Boccia for her assistance with the translations. Unless noted otherwise, all translations from Italian are by the author.

1 The "standard narrative" is outlined principally by Siegfried Giedion in *Space, Time, and Architecture* (Cambridge: Harvard University Press, 3rd ed. 1954) and Nikolaus Pevsner in *An Outline of Western Architecture* (Harmondsworth: Penguin Books, 1977), and *Pioneers of Modern Design* (Harmondsworth: Penguin Books, 1975). An incisive critique of this view of modern architectural history is offered by David Watkin in *Morality and Architecture* (Oxford: Clarendon Press, 1977).

2 Among more recent and sympathetic critical appraisals of the traditional architecture of the inter-war period, see Ettore Maria Mazzola, ed., *Controstoria dell'architettura moderna: Roma 1900-1940/Counter History of Modern Architecture: Rome 1900-1940* (Florence: Alinea Editrice, 2004), pp. 114-118; Terry Kirk, *The Architecture of Modern Italy: Volume II: Visions of Utopia, 1900-Present* (New York: Princeton Architectural Press, 2005); Mario Pisani, *Architetture di Marcello Piacentini: le opera maestre* (Rome: Clear, 2004); and Marina Docci and Maria Grazia Turco, eds., *L'architettura dell' "altra" modernità* (Rome: Gangemi, 2010) (hereafter Docci and Turco). While interest has burgeoned recently among some architectural historians in Italy, anecdotal experience suggests it still has not significantly affected the attitudes of architects and professors of architectural design, who remain overwhelmingly committed to the modernist narrative.

3 See Paolo Micalizzi, "L'altra modernità di Armando Brasini," in Docci and Turco, pp. 416-17. For a review of critical reception of Brasini and recent scholarship, see Elisabetta Procida, ed., *La sede storica dell'INAIL a Roma: Il palazzo in via IV Novembre* (Milano: Tipolitografia INAIL, 2009), pp. 19-35 (hereafter Procida, *La sede*). Brasini's work has been included for several years in courses offered at the Rome Studies Program of the University of Notre Dame taught by Professor Ettore Maria Mazzola. Several of Brasini's most important projects were located outside of Rome, for example, in Paris, Foggia, Taranto, and in Libya, but these are beyond the scope of the present essay. Brasini's projects for Albania were discussed in the conference "Architetti e Ingegneri Italiani in Albania" held in Tirana in December 2011.

4 Luca Brasini, *L'opera architettonica e urbanistica di Armando Brasini dall'Urbe Massima al Ponte sullo Stretto di Messina* (Rome: [s.n.], 1979), p. 12 (hereafter Brasini, *L'opera*). Luca Brasini includes an autobiographical text by his father pp. 12-30. Additional biographical information is available in Procida, *La sede*, pp. 19-35, and in Mario Pisani, *Architetture di Armando Brasini* (Rome: Officina edizoni, 1996) (hereafter Pisani, *Brasini*).

5 For the Giardino Zoologico entrance, see Pisani, *Brasini*, p. 29. The Piazza Navona project is illustrated in Pisani, *Brasini*, p. 9. The long and complex relationship between Brasini and Piacentini awaits new scholarship to be better understood.

6 For a detailed history of the project, see Elisabetta Frascaroli, "La complessa vicenda di un monumentale palazzo," in Procida, *La sede*, pp. 65-89.

7 Roberto Dulio, "Zevi/Brasini/Zevi," in Procida, *La sede*, pp. 37-43, p. 40.

8 Frascaroli, in Procida, *La sede*, p. 66.

9 Brasini, *L'opera*, p. 135 and Procida, *La sede*, pp. 15-16.

10 Pisani, *Brasini*, pp. 80-85.

11 Luigi Prestinenza Puglisi, "Imparare da Brasini" in Procida, *La sede*, pp. 159-165, p. 163.

12 For background on the exposition and the "Tavola degli Orrori," see Terry Kirk, *The Architecture of Modern Italy: Volume II: Visions of Utopia, 1900-Present* (New York: Princeton Architectural Press, 2005), pp. 81-83, and Procida, *La sede*, pp. 21 and 104. The same year,

Mussolini himself characterized the INAIL building in a speech before the Italian Senate as "an industrial accident befalling the National Insurance Institute for the Prevention of Industrial Accidents," as quoted in Pisani, *Brasini*, p. 80.

13 Brasini's entry to the Palace of the Soviets competition of 1931, with its pyramidal mass supporting a colossal statue of Lenin, apparently angered Mussolini and contributed to Brasini's fall from official favor. See Brasini, *L'opera*, pp. 68-70; Gian Paolo Consoli, "Storia di un tentativo: committenza, progetto e costruzione del ponte Flaminio di Armando Brasini 1930-1950," in Docci and Turco, pp. 433-439, p. 435; Procida, *La sede*, pp. 27-28; and Pisani, *Brasini*, pp. 10-11.

14 Brasini's privileged position among the architects favored by the regime in the 1920s (among other honors, Brasini was elected to the Royal Academy of Italy) quickly faded after 1931. See Consoli, in Docci and Turco, p. 436; see also Giampaolo Consoli, "Roma, Foggia, Taranto: Stile di Armando Brasini," in Claudio D'Amato Guerrieri, ed., *Città di Pietra/Cities of Stone* (Venice: Marsilio Editori, 2006), pp. 57-58; Procida, *La sede*, p. 27; and Pisani, *Brasini*, p. 12.

15 Brasini, *L'opera*, p. 23 and Consoli, "Roma, Foggia, Taranto: Stile di Armando Brasini," p. 59.

16 Venturi, 1977, p. 92. See also Pisani, *Brasini*, pp. 104-117.

17 Franco Borsi, quoted in Procida, *La sede*, p. 25.

18 Brasini, *L'opera*, pp. 118-121.

19 *Ibid.*

20 The model is still displayed inside the church of Sant'Ignazio, Rome. See also Brasini, *L'opera*, pp. 13, 54-58. The Sacro Cuore also still displays the architect's plaster model for the intended dome of that church.

21 Robert Venturi, "Armando Brasini Revisited," in his *Iconography and Electronics upon a Generic Architecture* (Cambridge: MIT Press, 1996), pp. 59-61; also quoted in Procida, *La sede*, p. 25.

22 Procida, *La sede*, p. 25.

23 This remains an important distinction: for Renaissance architects like Palladio and, later, those making the Grand Tour in the eighteenth and early nineteenth centuries, measuring Roman ruins was a source of knowledge of classical architecture and detail; in the latter half of the nineteenth century and into the twentieth, the ruins were seen as valuable precisely for their ruined state. Compare, for example, the graphic reconstructions of the École des Beaux-Arts *pensionnaires* in Rome with the sketchbooks of Le Corbusier and Louis Kahn.

24 See below, in discussion of his plan for the Campo Marzio. For more about the Museo and Brasini's work on the Vittoriano, see Pisani, *Brasini*, pp. 63-67.

25 Brasini, *L'opera*, p. 16.

26 *Ibid.*

27 These two terms are taken from the Secretary of the Interior's Standards for Rehabilitation, National Park Service, Washington, DC, 1977, revised 1995 (available online at *http://www.nps.gov/hps/tps/standguide/rehab/rehab_standards.htm*), which have served as a *de facto* national historic preservation policy since their inception. See Steven W. Semes, *The Future of the Past: A Conservation Ethic for Architecture, Urbanism, and Historic Preservation* (New York: W. W. Norton & Co., 2009), pp. 137-39 and 168-71.

28 One can see similar progressive editing of detail and emphasis on the power of abstract masses in contemporary designs by the classicists Edwin Lutyens and Paul Cret, or the Gothicists Giles Gilbert Scott and Bertram Goodhue.

29 Mario Pisani, "L'architettura di Armando Brasini: dal Barocco magniloquente alla progressiva semplificazione del linguaggio," in Docci and Turco, pp. 425-431.

30 Brasini was not unaware of or uninfluenced by contemporary modernist designers. See discussion of this issue throughout Docci and Turco, in particular by Micalizzi, in Docci and Turco, p. 421. The Banca di Lavoro in Naples and some unbuilt projects show that Brasini was not only aware of contemporary modernism, but tried his hand at it—perhaps deciding that it did not suit his particular abilities. See Brasini, *L'opera*, pp. 63-64 and 330-331 and Pisani, Brasini, pp. 12-14.

31 Brasini's interest in historic construction materials and methods, not just forms and stylistic treatment, led him to experiment with the ancient Roman technique of *opus testaceum* in his Palazzo del Podestà in Foggia, 1928-33. See Pisani, in Docci and Turco, p. 431.

32 Brasini, *L'opera*, p. 118 and Consoli, in Docci and Turco, p. 433.

33 Paolo Orano, *L'urbe massima: l'architettura e la decorazione di Armando Brasini* (Rome: A. F. Formiggini, 1917).

34 On "revolutionary architecture" in late eighteenth-century France, see Emil Kaufmann, *Three Revolutionary Architects: Boullée, Ledoux, Lequeu* (Philadelphia: American Philosophical Society, 1952). See also Pisani, in Docci and Turco, p. 429.

35 See Terry Kirk, "Framing Saint Peter's: Urban Planning in Fascist Rome," *The Art Bulletin*, vol. 88, no. 4, December 2006, pp. 756-776; see also Leonardo Benevolo, *San Pietro e la città di Roma* (Rome and Bari: Laterza, 2004) and Paolo Marconi, *Il recupero della bellezza* (Milano: Skira, 2005), pp. 94-100.

36 Carlo Francesco Dotti (1670-1759) was an important architect of the Baroque in Bologna whose best-known work is the Santuario della Madonna di San Luca, completed in 1743. The hilltop church is approached through a series of ramped arcades that begin with the monumental Arco del Meloncello and wind their way up the hill to the church.

37 After presenting his project of over thirty years earlier to the Vatican in 1948, Brasini received a reply from Cardinal Giovanni Battista Montini (later elected Pope Paul VI) that the review of the scheme by the competent officials "leaves no hope that, in the present state of things, your study could have any practical application." Brasini, *L'opera*, pp. 151-152.

38 Consoli, in Docci and Turco, pp. 433-39.

39 Armando Brasini, *Sistemazione del Campo Marzio, la via Imperiale, il foro Mussolini*, (Rome: [s.n.], 1927). Some of this material was published in the catalog of the exhibition "Armando Brasini: Roma Imperiale," at the Edmonton Art Gallery, 1977, cited in Note 2.

40 Brasini, *L'opera*, p. 23.

41 The full text and multiple illustrations of Brasini's plan are reprinted in Brasini, *L'opera*, pp. 76-107.

42 See Brasini's letter to Ugo Ojetti, reprinted in Brasini, *L'opera*, p. 103.

43 Procida, *La sede*, p. 27. Giovannoni, too, without naming Brasini, lamented the "megalomaniac" schemes around the Pantheon; see Gustavo Giovannoni, *Il quartiere romano del rinascimento* (Rome: Edizioni Della Bussola, 1946), p. 59. Brasini himself denied this characterization of his schemes, noting that many of his proposals were implemented by other architects. See Procida, *La sede*, p. 27.

44 Brasini, *L'opera*, p. 23.

45 Compare Brasini's plans with the plans of Imperial Roman public spaces documented in Filippo Coarelli, *Rome and Environs: An Archeological Guide* (Berkeley: University of California Press, 2007).

46 On the Baroque city, see Spiro Kostof , *The City Shaped* (New York: Bulfinch Press, 1991), especially Chapter 4, "The Grand Manner," pp. 209-277; and Joseph Connors, "Alliance and Enmity in Roman Baroque Urbanism," *Römisches Jahrbuch der Bibliotheca Hertziana*, 25, 1989, pp. 207-294.

47 Brasini, *L'opera*, p. 81-82.

48 For the exhibition at Villa Borghese, see Pisani, *Brasini*, pp. 41-43.

49 Brasini, *L'opera*, pp. 189-195, Frascaroli, in Procida, *La sede*, p. 65, and Gian Paolo Consoli, "Dal Primato della Citta' al Primato della Strada: Il Ruolo del Piano di Armando Brasini per Roma nello Sviluppo della Citta Fascista" in *L'architettura delle citta' italiane del XX secolo: dagli anni venti agli anni ottanta* (Milan: Editoriale Jaca Book, 2003), pp. 203-209.

50 See Arthur Drexler, ed., *The Architecture of the Ecole des Beaux-Arts* (New York: Museum of Modern Art, 1977), Donald Drew Egbert, *The Beaux-Arts Tradition in French Architecture* (Princeton: Princeton University Press, 1980), and Daniel Burnham and Edward H. Bennett, *Plan of Chicago* (New York: Da Capo Press 1970).

51 See Valter Vannelli, *Roma, architettura: la citta tra memoria e progetto* (Rome: Kappa, 1998), pp. 291-292. Vannelli points out that some of Brasini's proposals, such as the street linking St. Peter's to the Castel Sant'Angelo, dated back to the first *piano regolatore* of 1873 in which an "academic" approach was applied to the problems of mobility and communication throughout the city.

52 For Sant'Elia see Luciano Caramel, *Antonio Sant'Elia: The Complete Works* (New York: Rizzoli, 1988); for Ferriss, see Jean Ferriss Leich, *Architectural Visions: The Drawings of Hugh Ferriss* (New York: Whitney Library of Design, 1980). For modern abstraction's influence on Brasini see Micalizzi, in Docci and Turco, p. 421 and Pisani, *Brasini*, p. 12.

53 Piero Spagnesi, "Roma 1921-43: I concorsi di architettura," in Docci and Turco, pp. 363-366.

54 See Gustavo Giovannoni, *Vecchie citta' ed edilizia nuova* (Turin: Unione Tipografica Editrice Torinese, 1931). For Camillo Sitte, see George R. and Christiane Crasemann Collins, *Camillo Sitte: The Birth of Modern City Planning* (New York: Dover Publications, 1986).

55 Gustavo Giovannoni, quoted in Procida, *La sede*, p. 89, note 224; see also Giovannoni, 1946, p. 59; and Carlo Ceschi, *Teoria e storia del restauro* (Rome: Mario Bulzoni Editore, 1970), p. 114.

56 Ugo Ojetti's letter is reprinted in Brasini, *L'opera*, pp. 103-105.

57 For example, see Paul Goldberger, "Triangulation," *The New Yorker*, December 19, 2005, pp. 98-100. Goldberger writes that the motive for preservation in the United States was often "not so much love of what is being preserved as fear of what will replace it. No wonder people feared the new forty years ago; architects were giving them every reason to."

58 Quoted in Robert C. Fried, *Planning the Eternal City: Roman Politics and Planning Since World War II* (New Haven: Yale University Press, 1973), pp. 31-32.

59 Procida, *La sede*, pp. 27, 29, and 34, note 108. The extent to which Brasini helped shape Mussolini's urban program, between 1925 and 1931, is not clear and we await further scholarly investigation on this critical issue.

60 Guglielmo Bilancioni, quoted in Procida, *La sede*, p. 27.

61 See Ghirardo, "Italian Architects and Fascist Politics," for a thorough review of the relations between style and politics under Fascism in Italy; see also Procida, *La sede*, p. 29.

62 See Ghirardo, "Italian Architects and Fascist Politics", regarding the Duce's ambivalence toward the competing stylistic camps. In contrast to the claims by Zevi and others that the fascist regime favored classical design and suppressed the Rationalists, it is now established that the relations between the regime and the stylistic camps were more complex. The apparent triumph of the modernists was officially registered in 1938 with a decree by the Ministry of Public Instruction prohibiting the use of historical styles in either restoration or new construction. See Ettore Maria Mazzola, ed., *Controstoria dell'architettura moderna: Roma 1900-1940/Counter History of Modern Architecture: Rome 1900-1940* (Florence: Alinea Editrice, 2004), p. 82.

63 The unwillingness of the Fascist regime to support a "state style" of architecture is now widely recognized, though characterization of the classical architecture of the period as "fascist" persists. See also Terry Kirk, *The Architecture of Modern Italy: Volume II: Visions of Utopia, 1900-Present* (New York: Princeton Architectural Press, 2005), pp. 137-141.

64 See Ghirardo, "Italian Architects and Fascist Politics," concerning the pluralism and versatility of even the modernists and Rationalists in actual practice (especially pp. 118-119 and 126, note 73). She concludes by paraphrasing Edoardo Persico: "taste was the only issue that separated Rationalists from other Italian architects in Fascist Italy." Brasini's personal rapport with Mussolini was complicated and Brasini is described by contemporaries as lacking the political savvy that propelled his rival Piacentini into the position of principal architectural advisor to the regime in the 1930s. See Procida, *La sede*, pp. 27-30 and Puglisi, in Procida, *La sede*, pp. 160-161.

65 Pisani, in Docci and Turco, p. 429. A similar sentiment is expressed by Consoli in "Roma, Foggia, Taranto: Stile di Armando Brasini," in Claudio D'Amato Guerrieri, ed., *Città di Pietra/Cities of Stone* (Venice: Marsilio Editori, 2006), p. 60, describing Brasini's work as "a celebration of architecture as a constant discipline outside of any time."

66 Procida, *La sede*, p. 25.

67 See Gabriele Tagliaventi, et al., *The Other Modern/ L'altra modernità* (Savona: Dogma, 2000), and Docci and Turco.

68 Consoli, "Roma, Foggia, Taranto: Stile di Armando Brasini," p. 57.

From the Academies

Anniversary Observations on Education at the ICAA

By Paul Gunther

I n the 20 years since the establishment of the formerly named Institute for the Study of Classical Architecture, and the ten since its formal alignment with Classical America in 2002, the recently rebranded Institute of Classical Architecture & Art (ICAA) has extended its core teaching role in two essential ways: Building on past offerings and creating new platforms.

Even as there is an endless supply of worthy new initiatives, our progress is necessarily deliberate and methodical. We prudently extend institutional focus on prospective next steps and growth, when and if combined income and the constituent marketplace fit our mission intent and allow us to do so. Change for change's sake is not and never will be our strategic pathway. There is already much to be proud of and much therefore to strengthen; in my view, it is our privilege and duty as sole contemporary stewards of the classical tradition. I am delighted therefore to have the opportunity to describe our pedagogical goals here.

Continuing education best exemplifies our future as enlivened by a core curriculum consisting of theory, manual skills, and practice conveyed by uniquely qualified instructors. Driving the growth of this core above all has been the outreach of the 15 chapters, whose frontline recruitment of and engagement with new constituents describe a commensurate and concomitant demand for education in classical design. The opportunity to recruit

and certify regional mentors with the necessary training becomes an ever-greater one. At present, the cooperation of the national staff and education committee working with the chapter volunteers is the cohesive force that lends the strength and encouragement to expand.

Alongside elective course offerings are the *periodic intensive programs* currently offered from the Henry Hope Reed Classroom at national headquarters in New York. The intensives consolidate the core curriculum in ten 15-hour days including field trips and studio time scheduled amidst a dense array of lectures. To begin offering these intensives at chapter locations emerges as a key strategic goal. The growing *library* as well as the *historic plaster cast* collection are becoming ready resources to all. A reinvigorated *Certificate in Classical Architecture* means that those completing the core curriculum in its full rigor gain a permanent recording of their accomplishments, the value of which is acknowledged by clients, fellow practitioners, and builders alike. The rigorous annual *drawing tour* to Rome each year is the foremost travel aspect of CE. Favoring them all is the ever-growing sophistication defining acceptable content of AIA *"continuing education hours"* (as presently labeled); our full CE repertory reminds students as well as AIA decision-makers that the ICAA best addresses the cultural memory of design as an applicable modern tool.

The advent of the *Grand Central Academy of Art* in 2005 as the division of the Institute focused on architecture's sister arts in drawing, painting, and sculpture has since fulfilled an essential aspect of the mission statement.

Artist and trustee, Jacob Collins, led the way in terms of curriculum and initial recruitment from a strong community of young artists in search of the rigorous classical training scornfully abandoned by leading art schools long ago. As the Grand Central Academy instruction requires the plaster casts and live model studios consolidated at 20 West 44th Street, its teaching is inherently tethered to the headquarters location even as the audience served is countrywide and beyond. A challenging three-year core program thrives along with a summer landscape painting fellowship, regular *concours* across artistic disciplines, and special evening, weekend, and summer workshops together constitute a dynamic complement to the design education framing the balance of ICAA education.

The foremost and most recent achievement is the *Beaux-Arts Atelier (BAA)*, which makes manifest a strategic goal that has been in place since the creation of the Institute: A full-time one-year course of study that consists of 70-hour weeks guided by the core instructors and visiting experts who all draw from the resources available at the national office. Upon completion, students receive a *Beaux-Arts Atelier Certificate,* which in the early twenty-first century is unique in the world. This program is the culmination to date of

Collaborative analytiques by 2011-12 BAA students: Figure 1 (opposite) by David Markel and Nina Roefaro Lomeo. Figure 2 (page 64) by Syreeta Brooks and Ryan Hughes. Figure 3 (page 65) by Mark Hendricks, Susanne Smith, and Peter Spalding.

BEAUX-ARTS ATELIER

2011 - 2012

MDCCLXXXIX FEDERAL HALL

Corinthian capitae, geometric study, 2012
(with S. Bass) 10" x 12"

our essential purpose and its dividends bind all else we do exemplified by the dissemination of qualified teachers nationwide and comprehensively trained designers for all nature of professional practice and related craft and building arts. Its focus and energy give meaning to all our efforts. To our delight, crossover instruction and classroom time with the Grand Central Academy means another step in rebuilding the essential inter-disciplinary spirit of classicism. Over time, the BAA might extend to a multi-year program of study; for now, however, focus is on institutionalizing the effort under way.

Another dividend is the prospect for *curriculum-sharing partnerships with innovative accredited schools of architecture* daring to go outside the now century-old boundaries of modernism in shared recognition of the demands of the marketplace for both practice and public expectation. Such discussions are

emerging today, inspired in part by the successful pilot four years past with the School of Architecture at the Georgia Institute of Technology.

Accreditation as a freestanding school of architecture and design is not a present ICAA goal. Instead, it is nimble extension of established educational offerings and partnership models accompanied by a selective addition of new platforms when possible to execute with concurrent capacity.

One such platform—technology—is never far from our minds as evident in progress so far on the web site, blog, and regular programmatic updates that occur daily given our national scope. We are aware of the constant array of online options ranging from a full-fledged certificate-training program to the streaming of public lectures whether live or in sequential archives. We appreciate the constant shifts in and increased capacities of such

opportunities. We strive to take tactical advantage and add them to our overall educational arsenal.

Nonetheless, as history teaches us, the successful outcome of direct contact of mentor to apprentice is guided above all by the refinement of observation and best demonstrated by the hand recording on paper. Thus by our defining nature, technology is and will be deployed only when subservient to the humanity endemic to classicism itself. It must remain a means to that end and not an end in itself—another privilege and duty that is ours uniquely.

On this anniversary year, I salute all the teachers, students, and generous friends who have propelled this work forward.

Paul Gunther is President of the Institute of Classical Architecture & Art.

Figure 4 (opposite left): Design for door for Federal Hall by Nina Roefaro.

Figure 5 (opposite right): Geometrical study of Corinthian capital by Nina Roefaro.

Figure 6 (left): St. Patrick's Church, New York City, by Susanne Smith.

Figure 7 (page 68): Santa Maria di Loreto, Rome, by Peter Spalding.

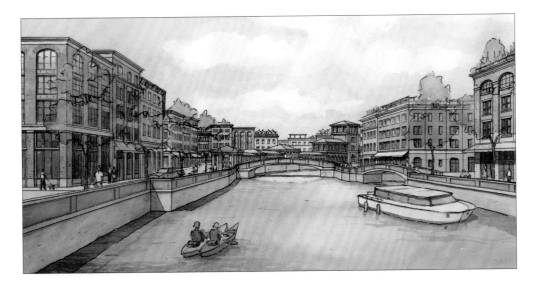

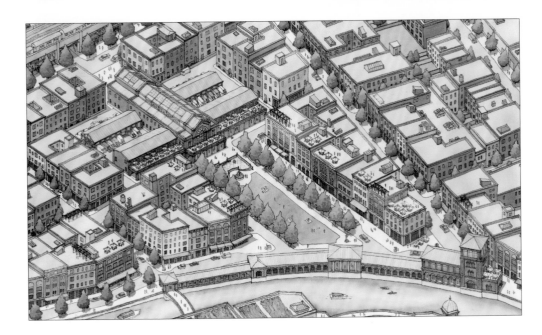

UNIVERSITY OF NOTRE DAME
Second Year Graduate Studio
Spring 2011

INSTRUCTORS:
Philip Bess
Samir Younés

PROJECT: Master plan, Gowanus, Brooklyn, New York

For their graduate theses, spouses Jennifer and John Griffin jointly developed a master plan for the Gowanus neighborhood in Brooklyn. An active industrial and shipping center since the 1860s, Gowanus is zoned for light to mid-level manufacturing. Rumors of rezoning inspired the project because the Griffins believe that the integration of community and industry is crucial to the revitalization of the neighborhood. In her thesis, Jennifer explored how local agriculture and public marketplaces are critical components of flourishing cities, while John focused on how industrial activity could be incorporated within a pedestrian friendly, mixed-use, and socially diverse neighborhood.

Opening figure (pages 60-61) and figures 1-3 (left): Redevelopment, Brooklyn, New York, perspectives by Jennifer and John Griffin.

UNIVERSITY OF
NOTRE DAME
Architecture and the Building Arts Concentration
Spring 2010-11

INSTRUCTOR:
Kevin Buccellato

PROJECT: Architectural details and models
The Building Arts concentration, a component of the Notre Dame School of Architecture's undergraduate curriculum, began in 2009 and focuses on designing and constructing architectural details and models. Under the direction of Professor Kevin Buccellato, it is a four-course sequence designed to develop a keen sense of detail and foundational understanding of methods of assembly. All courses involve team projects. The first part of the concentration spans two semesters during which students research a historically significant building to produce authoritative drawings and build a detailed model at an appropriate scale. In the third and fourth semesters the team designs and builds, at full scale, a traditional architectural element such as a mantelpiece, stair, newel post, or balustrade.

Figure 1 (top): Building study model, Pennsylvania Station, New York, New York by Lauren Albergo, Marie Anne Cross Lopez, William Hull, Martin Wieck, and Camilla Zablah Jiminez.

Figures 2-4 (left): Corner condition study model, The Parthenon, Athens, Greece by Selena Anders, Joanna Bea, Tricia Bertke, Eric Bootsma, and Crystal Ohoh.

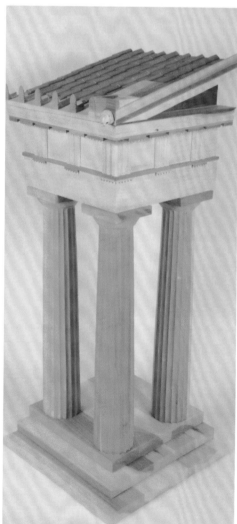

UNIVERSITY OF NOTRE DAME
First Year Graduate Studio
Spring 2011

INSTRUCTOR:
Richard Economakis

PROJECT: Master plan, Bath, United Kingdom
In this studio, first-year graduate students focused on the architectural past and future of the City of Bath, a World Heritage Site since 1987. The project was a continuation of the 2009 summer program that had outlined a master plan to address traditional urban patterns, building forms and constructional techniques of Bath's Western Riverside area. During the Spring 2011 semester, students focused on the improvement of a blighted section in the Kingsmead and Green Park neighborhoods, which fall within Bath's historic center to the west of the medieval abbey. The students examined the history and evolution of the city, especially during the Middle Ages and eighteenth century, and assessed the contemporary architectural needs of the area under study.

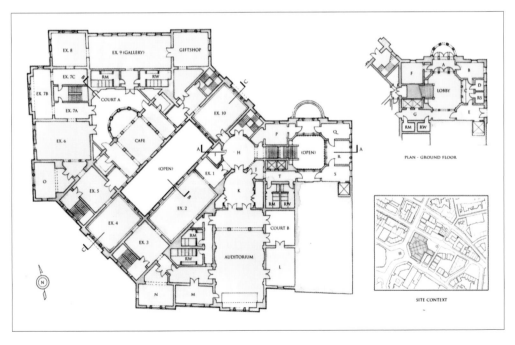

Figures 1-4 (above and left): Bath World Heritage Center, perspectives and plan by Ian Manire.

UNIVERSITY OF NOTRE DAME
Third Year Graduate Studio
Fall 2010

INSTRUCTOR:
David Mayernik

PROJECT: A Library, Rome, Italy
This library project for an urban site in Rome required students to provide a court-yard, living quarters for visiting faculty, and a Director's apartment in addition to the expected book stacks and reading rooms. Graduate student Keith Kirley chose to design his library as if for the American Academy in Rome, taking as his precedent a typical Roman Palazzo. The result therefore adapts a residential typology in order to accommodate an academic complex in the midst of the city. The primary reading rooms, including a rare book room, are located on the *piano nobile*.

Figures 1-3 (below and right): A Library, Rome, Italy, plan, section and elevation by Keith Kirley.

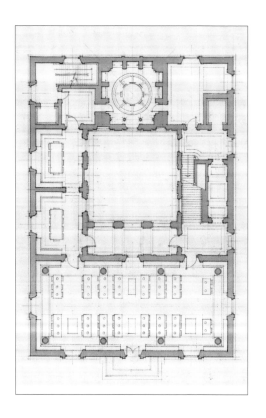

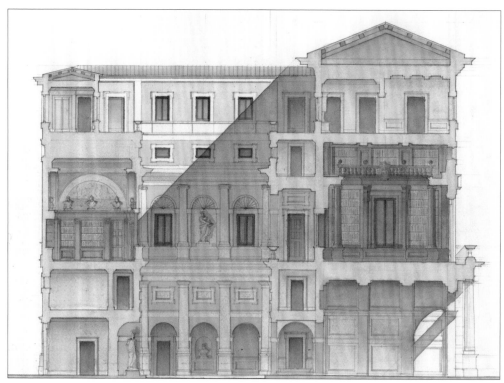

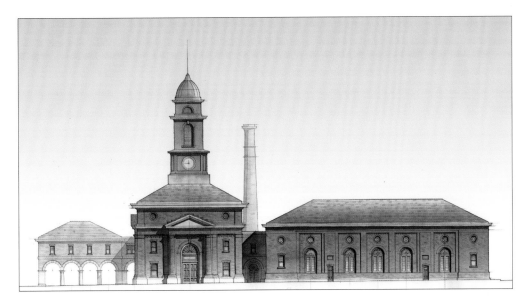

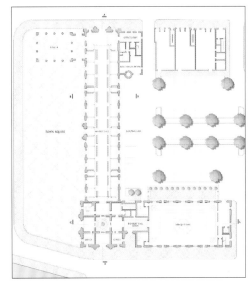

UNIVERSITY OF NOTRE DAME

Third Year Graduate Studio
Spring 2011

INSTRUCTOR:
Michael Lykoudis

PROJECT: Market, Prairie Crossing, Grayslake, Illinois

Prairie Crossing is a "conservation community" in Grayslake, Illinois, located within commuting distance by rail from Chicago and designed to allow the preservation of open land through responsible development practices. The proposed Farm Market for the community is a 35,000-square-foot civic and commercial center intended to exemplify the relationship between the local agriculture and sustainable architecture. Graduate student Keith Kirley chose this project because he wanted to explore the potential for public markets to promote economic development in master-planned communities.

Figures 1-3 (above and right): Market, Prairie Crossing, Grayslake, Illinois, perspective, plan, and elevation by Keith Kirley.

UNIVERSITY OF NOTRE DAME

Fifth Year Undergraduate Studio
Fall 2010

INSTRUCTORS:
Douglas Duany
Samir Younés

PROJECT: Vacation resort, Las Catalinas, Costa Rica

Students began this collaborative studio with a field trip to Costa Rica and Nicaragua to document the character of the local architecture. The proposed site for the resort town, *Guachepelines,* is perched on a high promontory overlooking the Pacific Ocean. Students were encouraged to develop a master plan to endure several centuries into the future. The town's public realm includes a market hall, a water tower, fountains, and a hierarchy of urban spaces. Its private realm includes hotels, fitness facilities, restaurants, and a variety of individual houses and private gardens. The project required that students study and demonstrate understanding of the town's urban, architectural, and tectonic characteristics. The project therefor consisted of three phases: An urban phase in which students collectively designed a master plan; an architectural phase in which each student individually designed at least two buildings; and a tectonic phase in which each student developed a three-dimensional constructional detail to illustrate materials and joinery.

Figure 1 (below): Plan by Paige Mariucci and Marty Sandburg.

Figure 2 (below): Market interior by Samantha Lopez.

Figures 3 and 4 (opposite top): Elevations by James Paul Hayes.

Figure 5 (opposite bottom): Collaborative aerial perpsective.

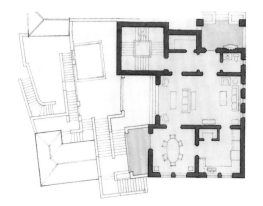

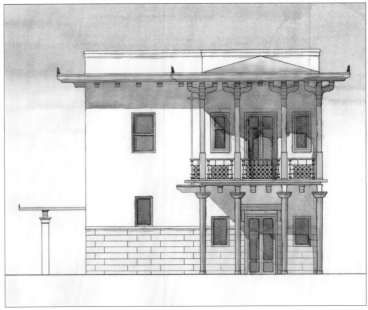

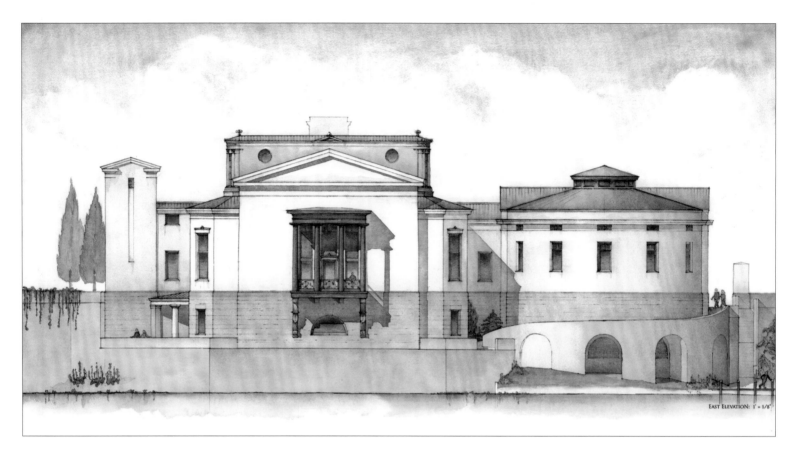

UNIVERSITY OF NOTRE DAME

Fifth Year Undergraduate Studio
Fall 2010

INSTRUCTOR:
Thomas Gordon Smith

PROJECT: Abolitionist Museum, South Bend, Indiana

Students were required to study the two interrelated aspects of American culture for which the Abolitionist Museum would be built: the Greek Revival and the Abolitionist Movement. Fifth-year student Matthew Brown found that the Greek Revival had a greater impact on the United States, both socially and geographically, beyond merely shaping the architectural vocabulary of the antebellum South. Brown's 60,000-square-foot design draws on precedents from ancient Greece and early nineteenth-century American architecture in ways that are completely compatible with modern building systems.

The main gallery is modeled after the interior of Iktinos' Temple of Apollo Epikourios at Bassai, which features the first known use of the Corinthian column and a unique interpretation of the Ionic order. The bronze tympanum sculpture above the main entrance incorporates the Liberty Bell as a powerful symbol of the Abolitionist movement.

Figures 1-3 (above, right, and below): Abolitionist Museum, South Bend, Indiana, section and elevations by Matthew Brown.

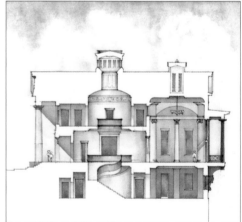

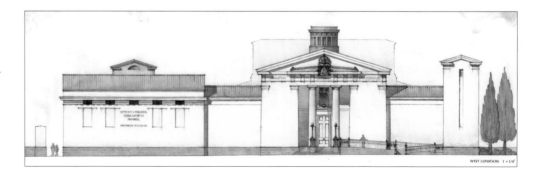

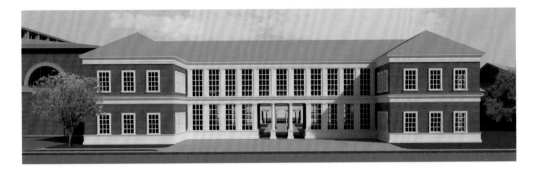

UNIVERSITY OF MIAMI

*Upper Lever Elective Studio: The Principles
of Classical Architecture*
Spring 2012

INSTRUCTOR:
Richard John

This studio departs from the usual format of a single design problem in order to study both the vocabulary (the orders) and the syntax (composition) of classical architecture through a number of smaller pedagogical exercises and esquisse problems. Students begin with the principles of composition and then study Paul Cret's method of program analysis before completing a Parallel of the Orders using original texts and treatises. After façade exercises based on Letarouilly, they undertake two design projects: first a three-teacher village schoolhouse and then a YMCA for a Naval Base in Manila.

Figure 1 (top): Administration and classroom building for YMCA, Manila, by Rocco Monaco.

Figures 2 and 3 (middle and bottom): Village schoolhouse, elevations and perspective by Rocco Monaco.

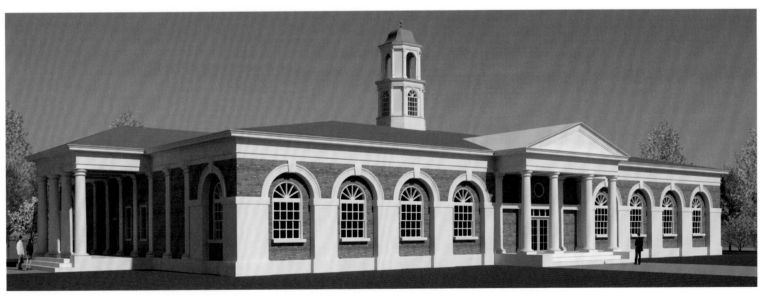

UNIVERSITY OF MIAMI
Graduate Studio in Rome
Spring 2011

INSTRUCTOR:
Alessandro Pierattini

PROJECT: Urbanization Project in Trastevere, Rome

For students spending a semester in Rome as part of the University of Miami's graduate program, the primary studio project in 2011 focused on an under-utilized site in Trastevere. After studying medieval Roman building typologies, in particular the form and construction of the casa in linea and casa a schiera types, students worked collaboratively to develop a masterplan for the Military Area at Via di San Michele, the former Orti del Convento di San Francesco. Subsequently each student developed proposals for individual buildings within the masterplan.

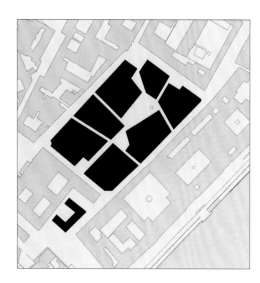

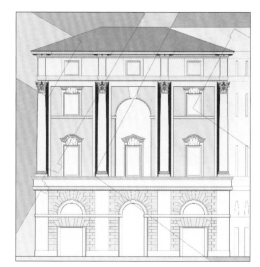

Figures 1 and 2 (top right): Collaborative masterplan of the site, and plan and elevation of an individual building by Kevin Hoffmann.

Figure 3 (right): Elevation by Tim Hayes.

Figure 4 (far right): Corinthian capital by Ruoyao Liu.

Figure 5 (below): Elevation of block by Lynette Mercado.

UNIVERSITY OF MIAMI
Graduate Studio in Rome
Spring 2012

INSTRUCTORS:
Alessandro Pierattini
Jean-François Lejeune

PROJECT: Reimagining the Ghetto of Rome
Students began by analyzing the Via dei Funari
(Street of the Cord-makers) from Largo
Arenula to the Piazza Campitelli at the foot
of the Campidoglio, focusing on pattern, typology, block size and shape, street widths, urban
sequence, the local character of spaces (piazze,
piazzette, larghi, and courtyards), and major
civic furniture (statues, fountains, drinking
fountains, etc.). The second phase, in the
tradition of "morpho-typological" studies,
involved students working in pairs to reimagine
the area around the synagogue, reconfiguring
the neighborhood into a place where contemporary public activities can take place through
a variety of building types and public spaces.

Lectures and site visits will illustrate the
urbanistic debates that raged in Rome from
the late 1800s to the early 1930s between the
proponents of a modern urban planning
technique (epitomized by the neighborhoods
around Termini, Piazza Vittorio Emmanuele
and Via Veneto) and the theories outlined by
Camillo Sitte in his book *Der Städtebau* (1889).

Figures 1 and 2 (left and above): Collaborative masterplan
and perspectival views by Jason Hill and Christopher
Stoddard.

JUDSON UNIVERSITY
Advanced Design Studios

INSTRUCTOR:
Christopher Miller

Judson University's liberal arts character and the rich student interest in ethical service shape Judson's architecture program. The curriculum works to integrate the diverse approaches of its faculty (including a value in the history of architecture in contemporary practice) and the importance of cultivating the tradition of urban environments. At present, opportunities for students to explore classical architecture and traditional urbanism are found in summer European study, in a civic architecture studio, in watercolor instruction, in a substantial history and theory curriculum at the undergraduate and graduate levels, and in independent and thesis projects.

Figure 1 (below): Proposal for Christ Church, Savannah, GA, perspective and site plan by Brian Mork.

Figures 2 and 3 (right top and middle): Proposal for a new Arts Center, Lochgelly, Scotland, perspectives by John Martin.

Figure 4 (opposite, bottom): Proposal for a new City Hall, Evanston, IL, perspective by Kevin Solomon.

Figure 5 (above): Proposal for a Symphony Hall, Fergus Falls, MN, perspective by Seth Holmen.

Figure 6 (below): Proposal for a new City Hall, Grand Rapids, MI, elevation by Rhyse Altman.

The Allied Arts

Grand Central Academy of Art

The Grand Central Academy of Art (GCA) at the ICAA offers classical training to serious students. Taught by professional, exhibiting artists, the GCA offers a positive environment for classical instruction in drawing, painting, and sculpture. The GCA is home to the following programs: the Water Street Atelier, a program in classical painting; the Sculpture Atelier, a program in classical sculpture; the Hudson River Fellowship, a summer landscape painting school in the Catskill Mountains; and the GCA's Drawing and Classical Figure Sculpture Competitions.

The goal of the Academy is to train a generation of highly skilled, aesthetically sensitive artists in the humanist tradition. The program is built on the skills and ideas that have come from classical Greece and Rome, the Italian Renaissance, and the Beaux-Arts tradition of the nineteenth century.

Further, the mission of the Grand Central Academy is to offer a public place for the revival of the classical art tradition, to foster and support a community of artists in pursuit of aesthetic refinement and a high level of skill and beauty. The Grand Central Academy of Art is an integral part of the ICAA whose mission is the advancement of classical art and architecture in America.

CAST DRAWING

Beginning Core Program students spend their first year in the Cast Hall learning to draw from the casts. Drawing from the antique cast, a classically rendered stationary object—using a limited palette under controlled light—teaches students to address the

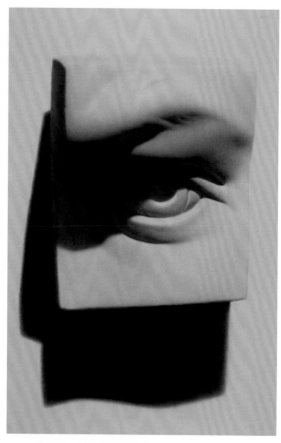

fundamental questions of composition, gesture, light direction, and value construction. Cast drawing encourages a slow, calm, thoughtful approach to gaining a deep three-dimensional understanding of the cast. Students are trained to think sculpturally, to make more accurate decisions, and to create drawings that are true to life.

Students are required to draw each feature cast (ear, eye, nose, and mouth)and at least one head and figure. Each student works at his or her own pace, generally to the end of the first year to complete excellent examples of each.

FIGURE DRAWING

Towards the end of the first year, students begin to draw the figure from life. Applying lessons learned by drawing the casts, they work on a series of linear figure drawings. The focus here is on accurate shapes, proportion, and dynamic gesture, without any finish or modeling. They move on to a series of drawings that show finished lines and clear resolution of detail. With their instructor's approval, students progress to drawing fully finished, modeled figures in month-long poses.

Drawing the figure through a series of long poses, students learn to manage relationships creating an analogous balance that describes the three-dimensional experience on the flat page.

Previous pages: "Lovers by the Waterfall" by Lauren Sansaricq, 2012, Oil on Panel, 32 x 24 in.

Figure 1 (opposite): "Eye Cast Study" by Rebecca Gray, 2012, Graphite on Paper, 18 x 24 in.

Figure 2 (left): "Saint Jerome" by Devin Cecil-Wishing, 2012, Graphite on Paper, 18 x 24 in.

Figure 3 (above): "Back Study" by Devin Cecil-Wishing, 2012, Graphite on Paper, 18 x 24 in.

Painting

As students gain fluency with the pencil, they may proceed to utilize these principles in paint. First, students work in grisaille (mono-chromatic painting in shades of gray) painting from the casts, copying master paintings, and then figures and portraits from life. Students showing facility in grisaille will progress to the use of a color palette. Students must produce at least six finished, excellent month-long-pose figure paintings in color to show mastery.

Sculpture

A traditional emphasis on clarity of form, simplicity of action, balance, and harmony are woven through the sculpture program. Meticulous copying of antique sculptures, rigorous study of anatomical figure structure (including a year-long study of écorché), and extensive modeling from life are emphasized.

Painting students are required to study sculpture alongside dedicated sculpture students. Likewise, sculpture students study cast and figure drawing and painting along-side painting students. Although all students are required to model casts, half-life-size figures, portraits, and an écorché, sculpture students go on to model a life-size torso and figure.

Ecorché is an advanced anatomical study of the human body as a whole. Students begin with an armature and sculpt the skeleton one bone at a time. Then the muscles are added layer upon layer as the human form is built up from the inside out. Study of the origin, insertion, and action of the muscles helps students develop an understanding of the body's overlapping forms and the portrayal of motion. Toward the end of the process, a live model is used to further the conception of the model's anatomy as a single system.

Figure 3 (opposite): "Portrait of Female" by Sam Hung, 2011, Graphite on Paper, 18 x 24 in.

Figure 4 (above): "Male Figure Study" by Brendan Johnston, 2012, Oil on Linen, 18 x 24 in.

The Hudson River Fellowship

The Hudson River Fellowship is intended to build a new movement of American art, modeling itself after the artistic, social, and spiritual values of the Hudson River School painters. It brings together the reawakening enthusiasm for the old American painters, the vigorous but unfocused scene of contemporary landscape painting, and the urgent need for a renewed reverence of the land. By bringing back the skills and spirit of the pre-impressionist landscape painters, the program gives direction to a new generation of painters. As the students learn to carefully study and reflect on the trees and clouds, blades of grass and cliffs, their paintings will become beautiful. Ideally, these artists and their representations of nature will help to lead the culture back to a stronger connection to the landscape. The fellowship seeks to make a contribution both to the art world and the conservation movement.

The Hudson River Fellowship is hosted by the Institute of Classical Architecture & Art in partnership with the Catskill Mountain Foundation's Sugar Maples Center for Creative Arts and is made possible by a leadership grant from the Morris and Alma Schapiro Fund.

Figure 5 (top): "Aroma" by Victoria Herrera, 2011, Oil on Board, 9 x 12 in..

Figure 6 (bottom): "Gumby, Pokey, and Spilled Gum Balls" by Sam Hung, 2012, Oil on Linen, 18 x 22 in.

Figure 7 (opposite left): "The Spirit of Freedom Upholding the Standard of Truth" by Niki Covington, 2012, Hydrocal, 30 x 12 x 10 in.

Figure 8 (opposite right): "Male Figure Study" by Patrick Byrnes, 2012, Graphite on Paper, 18 x 24 in.

Figure 9 (following pages, left): "Female Figure Study" by Brendan Johnston, 2012, Oil on Linen, 18 x 24 in.

Figure 10 (following pages, right): "Portrait Cast Study" by Sally Cochrane, 2012, Graphite on Paper, 18 x 24 in.

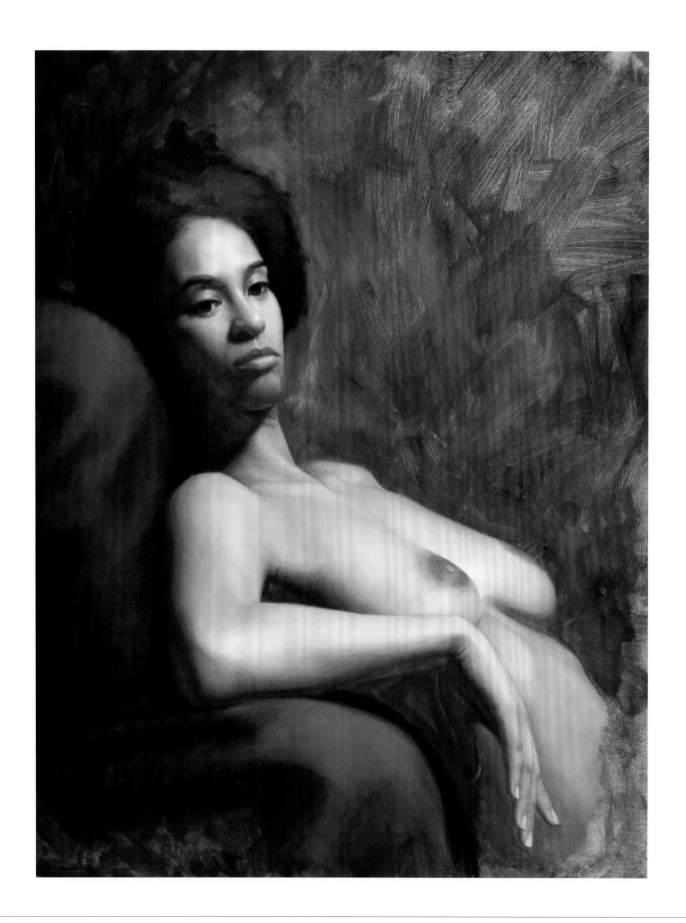

Miscellanea

Table in Rome

By Jana Vandergoot

Food is integral to understanding the urbanism of Rome. In the twenty-first century, as in antiquity, Rome functions as a consumer city, largely relying on the agriculture of the surrounding countryside for its food. This dependent relationship shaped a series of unique urban spaces, the hybrid character of which permeates not only the physical city but also its culture. I will explore some of the physical and cultural resonances of the journey that food makes from the fields to the city using the symbolic concept of Table (denoted in this essay with a capital "T" to distinguish it from the common noun.) Table is the city's striated fabric when it is activated by food: the landscape, buildings, streets, and piazzas are rich with the politics, social codes, and history of food. In Rome it has both a physical and cultural presence.

TABLE AS AN ALTAR ACTIVATED BY FOOD

The table has been considered a practical necessity in civic religion since the time of early Rome (753-509 BC) and was therefore given a special name: The *ara*, a Latin word usually translated into Italian as *altare* and into English as *altar*. The altar was the space upon which domestic and agricultural belief systems of the Latin Leagues gradually expanded to the life of the state and gave form to the early Roman government *(reggia)* and city *(urbs)*. Many ancient altars have been removed from their sites, or ground, and are now tucked away in museums. While this serves as protection, they are disconnected and lose a crucial component of their symbolic natures.

The visual language of worship that appeared in the pictorial ornament of altar tables was largely standardized, and this made it legible to the majority of people living in Rome. In *De Oratore* (III, i, 197) Cicero insists that everyone, even the least educated in the crowd, the *vulgus imperitorum*, should be able to understand works of art. Civic religion practiced by the priests and nobles in the government evolved from a familiar visual language initially developed for the fields and the rituals of rustic households. This language incorporated images of activities involving food: harvest, preparation, preservation, and sacrificial offerings to the gods. All of these activities made sense to the common people who routinely performed this work.

Offerings of food were determined by the particulars of time and place. Food was inevitably linked to seasonal weather, fertility cycles, the solar calendar, and perennial celebrations of a particular locality. Offerings of eggs, garlands of spring flowers, verdant foliage, or pomegranates bursting with crimson seeds were associated with fecundity, birth, and new life for the growing season. Grape must, salt, honeyed wine, milk, and water were used to celebrate lasting harvest, preservation, and perpetually healthy flocks. Boar, goat, lamb, and ox—animals that could feed hundreds of people in one sitting—were reserved for the most momentous occasions [FIGURE 3]. Aromatic olive branches, pine twigs, juniper and laurel were used as means of purification. Wheat or *mola salsa* (salted flour cakes) made of cereal grains were likely the most usual sacrificial offering. Staple crops were always appropriate and in most times they were also plentiful. Every household and market had them. As a result meal *(mola)* was often sprinkled on the offering or the altar. The act of sprinkling, "to put on the mola," is the root for the word *immolare* and eventually came to be used as the word for sacrifice in general.

The altar as locus point, as center, and the rituals of food sacrifice that accompany it compose a complex of layered meanings. Foods sacrificed on the altar are also depicted as ornament on the fabric of the altar [FIGURE 2]. Ornament is a visible sign that an altar has been used and that the *numen,* or spirit, has been called to the site through the offering of a divine meal, through the activity of Table. The food offerings on the table are evidence that the *numen* is present. A much-used altar might be full of actual floral garlands, animal bones, and fruit. These offerings would resonate with the images appearing in the ornamentation of the altar. An altar that was used often would have signs of wear, and these markings of the ritual event were themselves a form of ornamentation. This merging of ornament and event has profound implications for the idea of architectural ornament and the physical form that locus (center of activity) and ground (framework for activity) might take as they engage Table within and beyond the context of ancient Rome.

One small-scale, unlabeled outdoor altar can still be found between the Piazza Colonna and the *Ara Pacis* Museum. This altar is no taller than waist height and features fruit garlands, ox skulls, and a fire pit on its top [FIGURE 1]. It anchors the center of a small piazza, which carries the name "Field of Mars" (Campo Marzio). Archaeological maps of Rome reveal that an altar was present in many outdoor spaces and public forums and this network of altars allowed Table to expand across the city and into the daily activities of its inhabitants.

Two grand altars in particular articulate the character of the collective Table in ancient Rome: the Augustan Altar of Peace *(Ara Pacis Augustae)* and the Great Altar of Hercules *(Ara Maxima Herculis),* which were both centers of ritual activity inextricably tied to eating. The Altar of Peace has a powerful physical presence in modern Rome, housed in a museum designed by Richard Meier [FIGURE 4]. The Great Altar of Hercules, on the other hand, has left virtually no physical evidence. Its importance lies in the fact that through substantial historical documentation, speculation, and debate it can inform our current understanding of food systems in Rome.

AUGUSTAN ALTAR OF PEACE

On 4 July 13 BC, after a century of wars, the Roman Senate authorized the construction of an altar dedicated to peace under the rule of Augustus *(Pax Augusta).*

In ancient Roman religion an altar was the only structure required for a religious gathering. The *Ara Pacis* stood, without any accompanying temple, in an open floodplain that in the time of Augustus still fell outside of the city boundary. Through the Republic it was a place with many uses. It was Rome's hinterland for pasturing sheep. Soldiers and generals used it for military exercises, meals, and lodging. It was also the meeting place for foreign politicians not permitted to stay within the city proper.

The design of the altar incorporated many rural references, which appealed to the Roman nostalgia for pastoral living in times of peace. The altar fulfilled Augustus' vision of civic religion and represented a return to social mores. These mores were bound up with the notion that Roman ancestors were unified by a particular set of communal

Previous pages: Thermopolium, Ostia. Photograph by Dennis Jarvis.

Figure 1 (opposite): Altar in Piazza di Campo Marzio, Rome.

Figure 2 (above): Drawing of an ancient Roman altar by Nicholas Poussin. ©Trustees of the British Museum.

expectations. Carved into the marble of the Altar of Augustan Peace, therefore, are images of a bountiful earth, familial allegiance, and ritual piety [FIGURE 5]. Here, in the center of an urban space activated by food, the altar became Table.

The realistic representations of foods on the vegetal panels provided a compelling pictorial narrative for Roman citizens as they were recognized as essential components of their relationship to the land. Although not farmers themselves, they would recognize that the foods depicted on the panels determined the welfare of the state. David Castriota has argued that each plant depicted on the enclosure walls

represents its own sacred power or deity, and that this would have been apparent to Romans in the age of Augustus. In the sacred space of the Altar of Peace the laurel is Apollo, the vine is Liber (the Greek Dionysus), the wheat is Ceres (the Greek Demeter), and so forth. The floral imagery of the Altar of Peace most noticeably invokes the noble Apollo with whom Augustus personally associated himself. It also invokes the Aventine Triad, no doubt garnering the support of common people.

Within the modestly scaled enclosure, the altar table rests on an elevated podium; along the walls a series of weep holes were cut to allow sacrificial liquids to drain through the sloped floor out to the *Campus Martius,* the field dedicated to the Roman god of war, Mars. Thus sacred libations and animal sacrifices declared that a new life of peace would emerge from what was previously a place of war. This table furnished real food for the ritual act of collective eating. The zone of the altar is intimate and scaled to the human body. In contrast, a massive processional area spread out around it into the Field of Mars.

It is significant that the place Augustus chose for his altar lay along the major north-south road, the *Via Flaminia* (in modern Rome known as Via del Corso) [FIGURE 6]. The decision to construct major monuments here later contributed to the expansion of the city boundary to include the Field of Mars. This expansion changed the nature of the floodplain from the type of field that supported the feeding of animals and production of agriculture into another type of field, an urban framework able to support a series of civic centers.

In the context of the Altar of Peace, Table also possessed other signifiers, including the political maneuvering folded into ritual gatherings. Table was the locus, or center of gravity, which gathered crowds when activated by food. In twenty-first-century Rome, the governing Table remains very close to the place that Augustus chose for his Altar of Peace. The Piazza Colonna, situated on the ancient Via Flaminia, and the adjacent Piazza di Montecitorio, are only filled with people during political rallies. The reason is that on these piazzas we find the Palazzo Montecitorio, which houses the Chamber of Deputies, and the Palazzo Chigi, the official residence of the Prime Minister [FIGURE 7].

The Altar of Peace itself, after centuries submerged under four meters of waterlogged silt from the Tiber, was finally recovered in 1937, 2000 years after the birth of Augustus. Even in the twentieth century it served political purposes—Mussolini used the altar as a propaganda tool in 1938 when he tried to connect his dream of a modern empire with the grandeur of the Roman past through physical reconstruction of the city. The architecture of the Piazza Augusto Imperatore, which surrounds the *Ara Pacis* Museum and the Mausoleum of Augustus, is a powerful example of the fascist style [FIGURE 8]. Today, too, the altar continues to be used as a powerful political platform: Gianni Alemanno, on winning the mayoral election in 2008, announced that the new *Ara Pacis* Museum designed by Richard Meier should be dismantled.

THE GREAT ALTAR OF HERCULES

The Altar of Peace represents the Table of an Imperial family, but the activities of common people as they related to food also contributed to the character of the ancient network of altars. The lineage of the Great Altar of Hercules (*Ara Maxima Herculis*) can be traced to the city's "stomach," the flood-prone *Velabrum* valley where merchants and the

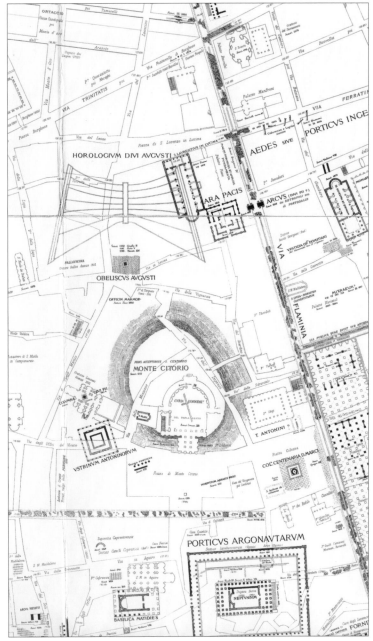

Figure 3 (opposite): Relief sculpture dating from 1st century AD depicting the Suovetaurilia—the sacrifice of a pig, ram, and a bull. Musée du Louvre, Paris.

Figure 4 (top left): The *Ara Pacis.* Photograph by Michael Day.

Figure 5 (left): Detail of the *Ara Pacis.* Photograph by Francesco Meschia.

Figure 6 (above): Location of the *Ara Pacis* in relation to the ancient *Via Flaminia.* Rodolfo Lanciani, *Forma Urbis Romae* (1893-1901).

soldier class imported, stored, and distributed food. The stomach was a center of hard work, and its messiness was tucked strategically out of sight of the political class. It was near this stomach that common Rome set its civic and sacred Table.

Literature dates the Great Altar of Hercules to 5-6 BC. It was located near the bend in the Tiber, which was also the location of the ancient *Forum Boarium* cattle market. The merchant and soldier class were admirers of the demigod Hercules, and they constituted a significant part of his cult membership. They are credited with the celebrations at the Great Altar in the fluvial crossroads that ultimately evolved into the *Forum Boarium*. No more fitting place in Rome for an altar to Hercules, the working man's ideal, could possibly be imagined.

A blocky podium grows from the deeply pitted volcanic rock that makes up the geological landscape of the Seven Hills of Rome. The horizontal *mensa*, a slab of the same volcanic *tufo* rock, expresses an affiliation to the demigod through the nature of its roughly hewn, earth-bound materiality. Ornamental reliefs on the altar speak to the mythic Labors of Hercules. The ancient Roman writer and scholar Varro (116-27 BC) wrote, "The first fruits of commercial goods are offered up on the Altar of Hercules…and every year [on August 12] the urban praetor sacrifices a heifer upon it on behalf of the state."

A massive *tufo* podium which forms part of the substructure of the church of Santa Maria in Cosmedin is, perhaps, the only surviving part of the Great Altar of Hercules [FIGURE 10]. The practice of recycling material from earlier structures was not uncommon in the history of Rome. From what is known about the altar, the social spectrum of those who shared in its events was much broader than was the case at many other altars. The festival of *Hercules Invictus* was on August 12 and 13. It began with a banquet for those who provided the offerings and likely included some honored guests such as senators or military generals. Later in the day all male citizens were able to join the festivities. This Table was more public than most of its kind. The celebrations continued until all of the meat presented in offering had been consumed. None was to be wasted.

The ground of an altar contributes as much to the meaning of the altar as its structure and ornament. Although we lack the evidence to describe properly the features of the Great Altar of Hercules, there is good reason to conclude that it was an outdoor altar. Outdoor altars were created for ritual consumption of food, typically involving animal sacrifice. The altar location and outdoor setting was thought to allow smoke and the aroma of sacrificial meat to rise and summon the *numen* of the god for which it had been prepared. Some altars that functioned on important religious feast days and involved animal sacrifice were positioned on axis with the portal of the *aedes* or temple. Through the portal, the god who resided within could witness the ritual that was taking place outside.

TABLE AS PRECINCT

The placement of the altar relative to a temple is convenient, but the *aedes* was not a necessity for the ritual sacrifice. Altars not positioned in front of a temple were structures standing alone in a sacred field or an urban area governed by a set of civic rules. The open area around the altar was referred to as the *templum*. The *aedes* remains as the most publically visible marker of antiquity in modern Rome, while the smaller structures of the altar network have been removed to museums, buried by silt, recycled into later constructions, ruined by war, or completely lost. The ruins of the *aedes* in Rome speak in an abstract or personified way of the deities and emperors they honor. However, in isolation, these edifices do not reveal the activities that took place around them and that were so essential to the significance of the field or ground in which the edifice stood. Thus the more nuanced meaning of Table as an entire precinct has been lost.

This gap in the story is registered in a shift that has occurred in the language used to describe the cultic activity of ancient Rome. The classic Latin word *templum*, from which the modern English word "temple" derives, originally referred to a precinct or field, rather than a singular edifice. The edifice is, in many instances, all that is left behind from the locus and ground of multi-layered meanings, which engendered the Table of ancient Rome.

There are other examples of the way in which the features of the precinct for an altar were determined by the nature of the deity it honored. In the case of the Augustan Altar of Peace food was placed on an elevated *mensa* (table). In the case of a chthonic deity, the altar was set within a subterranean pit in which offerings were consumed with fire. The *mundus*, which directly translates as "world", is described as a pit in the earth into which food was offered. Near the Great Altar of Hercules two of this subterranean type can be found: one for Ceres, the goddess of agriculture, and the other for Consus, protector of grain

Figure 7 (opposite): Palazzo Montecitorio, Rome, by Gian Lorenzo Bernini, 1653, and Carlo Fontana, 1694.

Figure 8 (below): Piazza Augusto Imperatore by Vittorio Ballio-Morpurgo, 1934-42. Photograph by Brett Holman.

storage and seed. In all cases the ground and the design of the altar reflect the nature of the god whom it revered. In the precinct of ancient altars, the Table activated ground and the Table *was* ground.

The Great Altar of Hercules knits together some of the most dynamic and richly layered geography in all of Rome. Virgil wrote of the Arcadians sacrificing to Hercules in front of the city in a *luco* (grove). The grove to which Virgil referred evolved to become the *Forum Boarium,* one of a series of *Venalium* forums that was dedicated to the exchange of food. Due to its location near the earliest river ford and cultural crossroads of the Tiber island, the *Forum Boarium* was a nexus of commerce and social activity, and thus it developed the characteristics of Table as a larger urban construct. In the *Forum Boarium* the idea of Table expands into the urban space of public forums. Landscape contours, forest succession, floods, droughts, river morphology, gatherings of people, herds of cattle, politically sanctioned calendar holidays, festivals, and tourist attractions give definition to the *Forum Boarium,* which occupies the valley between the Palatine, Aventine, and Capitoline Hills and extends to the east bank at the bend in the Tiber River. In the *Forum Boarium,* Table is ground; Table is a series of temporal harvest, storage, and feast events that characterize physical and cultural territory.

Traces remain of the Forum's role as a cattle market and its link to the agriculture of the *ager.* The *Arcus Argentariorum,* an arch built in 204 AD that is tucked into the bell tower of the seventh-century Basilica of San Giorgio in Velabro, has inscriptions referring to the *Forum Boarium* as well as a bas-relief carving of Hercules [FIGURES 9 AND 10]. Modern street placards make visible the name of the market, which in Italian is called Foro Boario. As the city limits expanded to encompass larger portions of land, so too the activities of the *Forum Boarium* moved further down river to Testaccio, the district through which much of ancient Rome's food supplies were brought from the port of Ostia. Here one finds the renowned nineteenth-century slaughterhouse that closed in the 1970s. In modern Rome, the presence of refrigeration facilities and chain supermarkets has largely replaced the need for a city slaughterhouse district. The disappearance of the urban cattle market in Rome, for better or worse, has resulted in a decrease in visibility for the complex rituals that accompany the consumption of meat. The Table formerly associated with the Altar of Hercules has become less of a permanent fixture in the fabric of the city and more of a narrative shaping modern Roman cuisine.

Interpreting the culture of ancient Rome by exploring altars that form the center of a precinct is quite different from interpretations focused on an edifice. Interpreting the precinct is more difficult because the ground has shifted dramatically through the millennia. This is even more problematic when trying to understand the horizontal field of altars spread across the city of Rome with each altar representing a surface that is an extension of the physical earthen floor. Altars were a way of elevating both the ground and the event of ritual. The scope of the metaphoric ground, which these altars both create and rest upon, is essential to the meaning of the ancient Roman Table. This idea is powerfully illustrated in the common practice in Augustan's time of putting a single turf (sod or grass from the earth) on an altar.

Robin Dripps, in her essay, "Groundwork," eloquently unpacks the idea of ground and describes it as, "the various patterns of physical, intellectual, poetic, and political structure that intersect, overlap, and weave together to become the context for human thought and action." Carrying her insight a bit further as it might apply to the altars of Roman civic religion, the altar network, the earthen floor that it engages, and the culture to which it gives expression might be understood as a multi-layered and multi-dimensional Table that creates Roman urbanism.

Many modern cities have an ambiguous relationship with food, with its distribution and processing taking place behind closed doors or tucked away in uncelebrated spaces, yet food is the lifeblood of cities. When designers and planners take the unifying concept of Table seriously, as can be seen in Rome, unity can be restored to the infrastructure and culture of a city. ⬿

The research for this essay was undertaken while Jana Vandergoot held the Institute of Classical Architecture & Art (ICAA) 2010 Rieger Graham Prize Affiliated Fellowship at the American Academy in Rome.

Figure 9 (above): The site of the *Forum Boarium* with the Arch of Janus Quadrifrons and the campanile of San Giorgio in Velabro. Drawing by Antonio Canaletto. ©Trustees of the British Museum.

Figure 10 (opposite left): Crypt of Santa Maria in Cosmedin, Rome, showing, through the doorway, the massive tufo blocks thought to be the only remains of the Great Altar of Hercules. Photograph by Holly Hayes.

Figure 11 (opposite right): Detail of the Hercules relief on the *Arcus Argentariorum.*

NOTES

1. Neville Morley, in his book *Metropolis and Hinterland*, discusses the nature of Rome as a consumer city that burdens the surrounding hinterlands with its need for food yet at the same time also stimulates its economy. Neville Morley, *Metropolis and Hinterland: The City of Rome and the Italian Economy 200 BC-200 AD* (Cambridge: Cambridge University Press, 1996), pp. 184-85. For discussion of Rome as a consumer city see also: Carolyn Steel, *Hungry Cities, How Food Shapes Our Lives* (London: Chatto & Windus, 2008).

2. Further discussion of the Latin Leagues involves the *feriae Latinae*, an annual religious event which supposedly brought together the heterogeneous Latin Leagues as a community and involved sacrifice on top of Mons Albanus. See T. P. Wiseman, "The city that never was: Alba Longa and the historical tradition", *Journal of Roman Archaeology*, 23, 2010, p. 435.

3. David Castriota, *The Ara Pacis Augustae and the Imagery of Abundance in Later Greek and Early Roman Imperial Art* (Princeton: Princeton University Press, 1995), p. 10. Castriota argues that the Roman populace understood the visual narrative of the Altar of Peace. Castriota references *De Oratore* and mentions that although Cicero was specifically referring to aesthetic response rather than judgment, it is unreasonable to assume that only the learned spectators were thought of as capable of judging programmatic content.

4. This list was developed from a study of the Roman festival calendar (the *Fasti Antiates* and *Fasti Praenestini*), holidays dedicated to gods and their respective ties to flora and fauna, as well as an understanding of the seasonal cycles of vegetable and animal produce of ancient Rome. See Wilhelmina Feemster Jashemski and Frederick Meyer, eds., *The Natural History of Pompeii* (Cambridge: Cambridge University Press, 2002).

5. For a discussion of the role of *mos maiorum* in early republican Roman society see W. G. Sinnigen and A. E. R. Boak, *A History of Rome to AD 565*, Sixth Edition (London: Macmillan, 1977), p. 87.

6. David Castriota, Ibid, p. 25. See also Giulia Caneva, *The Augustus Botanical Code. Ara Pacis: Speaking to the people through the images of nature*, (Rome: Gangemi, 2010).

7. The *Ara Pacis* was dedicated on 30 January 9 BC, a date which was subsequently celebrated as an official holiday with a sacrifice at the altar. L. Richardson, *A New Topographical Dictionary of Ancient Rome*, (Baltimore: The Johns Hopkins University Press, 1992), p. 208.

8. Joshua Arthurs, "Fascism as Heritage in Contemporary Italy," in Andrea Mammone and Giuseppe Veltri, eds., *Italy Today: The Sick Man of Europe* (London: Routledge, 2010), p. 114.

9. See Heidi de Mare and Anna Vos, eds., *Urban Rituals in Italy and the Netherlands* (Assen: Van Gorcum, 1993), p. 74. Vos discusses the "stomach" or "belly" of Rome as a distinct district along the Tiber.

10. See Annalisa Marzano, "Hercules and the triumphal feast for the Roman people" in I. B. Antela-Bernardez and T. Naco del Hoyo, eds., *Transforming Historical Landscapes in the Ancient Empires*, British Archaeological Reports International Series 1986, (Oxford: John and Erica Hedges, 2009), pp. 83-97.

11. Varro, *The Latin Language*, 6.54.

12. Lesley Adkins and Roy A. Adkins, *Handbook to Life in Ancient Rome*, (Oxford: Oxford University Press, 1998), p. 285.

13. Jörg Rüpke, ed., *Companion to Roman Religion*, (Oxford: Blackwell Publishing, 2007), p. 268.

14. See Sarah Iles Johnston, *Religions of the Ancient World: A Guide* (Cambridge: Harvard University Press, 2004), p. 278.

15. Denis Feeney, *Caesar's Calendar: Ancient Time and the Beginnings of History*, Sather Classical Lectures 65 (Berkeley: University of California Press, 2007), p. 161.

16. The general term for a food market was *forum venalium*. The *fora venalia* included the *Forum Boarium* (cattle), *Forum Holitorium* (vegetable, herbs, and oil), *Forum Piscarium* (fish), *Forum Suarium* (pork), *Forum Vinarium* (wine), and *Forum Pistorium* (bread), each area with its respective dedications to the gods.

17. For more reading on the social games and feasts that accompanied the cycles of food processing in the Testaccio district see De Mare and Vos, *Urban Rituals* cited above. See also Michael Ezban, "The Trash Heap of History" in *Places*: *http://places.designobserver.com/feature/rome-monte-testaccio-landfill-reclamation/33268/*.

18. Robert Maxwell Ogilvie, *The Romans and Their Gods in the Age of Augustus* (London: Chatto & Windus, 1969), p. 47.

19. Robin Dripps, "Groundwork" in Carol Burns and Andrea Kahn, eds., *Site Matters: Design Concepts, Histories, and Strategies* (New York: Routledge 2005), p. 59.

Why the Classical?
TWO DECADES OF TEACHING AT THE UNIVERSITY OF COLORADO AT DENVER: A RETROSPECTIVE GLANCE

By Taisto H. Mäkelä

Each generation needs to engage and develop its own version and interpretation of the classical tradition. By doing so, this vast and timeless tradition continues to serve the present. As Nietzsche commented in 1874, "I do not know what meaning classical studies could have for our time if they were not untimely—that is to say, acting counter to our time and thereby acting on our time and, let us hope, for the benefit of a time to come."

Student work from the University of Colorado at Denver was last published in *The Classicist* No. 1. Included was a model of the Tuscan Temple described by Vitruvius, which was completed in a class I taught in the fall of 1992. In the accompanying description, I explained my interest in classical architecture as a result of it being denied to me in my own education. This was, I suspect, because my teachers had never studied it themselves. As I'd written then, "We were all victims of an ignorance perpetuated by each generation of educators." When I arrived in Denver in 1989, however, I was intrigued to find two graduate students—Cameron Kruger and Warren Wick—completing design theses based on the classical tradition. Personally, I began to learn about classical architecture by teaching its principles beginning in a first year graduate design studio in the fall of 1990. This was later complemented by a seminar dedicated to ink washes, which began in 2003. Cameron Kruger, who went on to open his own practice, was kind enough to support my initiatives over these years and share his knowledge and passion for wash rendering with the students.

That first year studio began with an analysis of the Tuscan order. Through this analysis, the students began to comprehend the authority of the classical language. By fortunate coincidence, I found a fine example of a Tuscan Order in William Chambers' *A Treatise on the Decorative Part of Civil Architecture* (1791 edition). Students studied this order in terms of proportional relationships [FIGURE 9]. If, after careful analysis, a student had a convincing argument to change any of the proportional relationships of the Chambers Tuscan, they were allowed to do so. One student went so far as to carefully craft a two-foot tall wooden model of this order [FIGURE 1]. In the second exercise students used the width of their foot as the diameter at the base of the column. The students then produced a Tuscan order each scaled to their own body. Besides these proportional principles, the objectives of the studio were broad and included acquiring discipline in the language and systems of traditional design; utilizing the human body and its scale in design; understanding basic structural logic and architectonics; developing essential graphic and presentation skills; and gaining an appreciation of architecture as an essential constituent and manifestation of culture.

The student ink wash [FIGURE 3] is from the seminar I first taught in 2003. The seminar also explored the basic design concept of proportion as it relates to the history of architecture and how it can be utilized today. Students were required to show geometric construction lines using a scale based on the module of the column they had chosen. Everything was done with compass, straight edge, and proper drafting tools. No rulers or French curves allowed! Taking pride in a craft using the traditional materials was emphasized along with rigor and discipline as exemplified by the Beaux-Arts method.

Figure 1 (above): Wooden model of Tuscan order.

Figure 2 (opposite): Ink wash rendering by Kai Fishman.

Figure 3 (opposite top left): Ionic order by Heather Thigpen, 2005.

Figure 4 (opposite bottom left): Composite order by Michael Stephens, 2011.

Figure 5 (opposite right): Ionic order by Leslie Schneeberger. 2005.

Figure 6 (top left): Ionic order by D Manton Reiser, 2006.

Figure 7 (top right): Doric order by Jane Crisler, 2005.

Figure 8 (left): Corinthian order by Shana Beckham, 2006.

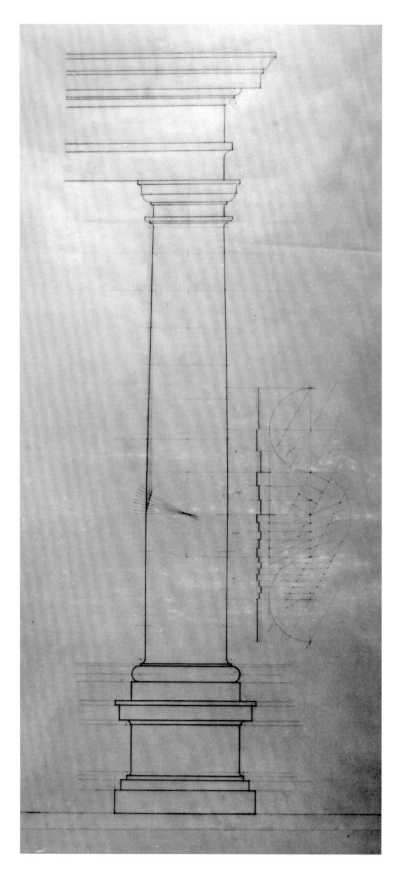

The wonderful thing about studying classical architecture is that by simply going through the exercises, the underlying logic and principles on which the work is based is revealed—classical architecture almost teaches itself. It is often difficult to get students to appreciate the clear and consistent exercise of logic but I have found that learning the orders is very helpful in this regard. What more basic tool is there for teaching architecture? Contemporary architectural design is essentially impoverished without an appreciation of the backdrop that the orders have provided through history.

Moreover, an appreciation of the classical tradition provides students with the intellectual and practical skills necessary to position themselves as discerning and critical thinkers in a particular sector of architectural practice, as well as within allied fields such as traditional urban design, preservation, the building arts, and interior and landscape architecture. The content of my courses provide theoretical inquiry with skill-based learning following the Beaux-Arts paradigm with the intention of providing a solid foundation for a successful professional career.

CAMERON KRUGER'S COMMENTS ON TEACHING HIS INK WASH SEMINAR:

By doing ink washes, students learn to see the underlying proportion of each order and the subtle differences between each version, of, say, the Ionic, whether it be Scamozzi's or from ancient Greece. They learn to see the personalities of previous architects articulated through a shared vocabulary. They also learn to see light revealing shape, for it is the ink-wash, the quintessential medium of the École des Beaux-Arts, that best expresses depth and richness of architectural form.

Each class begins with an introduction to the Classical Orders through the canonical texts: Vitruvius, Palladio, Vignola, and Chambers. The students work through the proportions. They learn guidelines but no agreed upon standards. They learn there are principles but no simple formulas.

Then the students begin to construct their own orders. They do this with traditional tools: pencils, compasses, paper, and dividers. As we discuss proportion and precedents, they begin to see possibilities. We start to study the composition in light, with charcoal or graphite. They draw the same order again and again, thinking about shadows, thinking about form and watch how the composition evolves.

Simultaneously, students are introduced to the ink-wash technique. They practice simple uniform washes on a watercolor block. They are hesitant at first, unable to see how forgiving the medium is. As we move to the graded wash they begin to develop confidence and can see the beauty of transparency. They learn that pitch black ink can become pure light falling on form. Through practice, their skill increases.

When the students begin the final drawing, they have studies and technique to build upon. With each careful wash layer upon wash, slowly building shade and shadow, the order comes into focus. The students learn to see what their predecessors saw one hundred years ago, two hundred years ago. They see things differently now;

when they walk down the street, buildings that were once mute speak to them. When they visit new cities, they recognize familiar forms. They are now part of a tradition. ❦

Prof. Taisto H. Mäkelä is Chair of the Department of Architecture at the University of Colorado, Denver.

Cameron P. Kruger, AIA, is the principal of Kruger Design-Build LLC and a Lecturer in the Department of Architecture at the University of Colorado

Figure 9 (opposite): Graphite drawing of Tuscan order after Chambers.

Figure 10 (left): Ionic order by Anne Shaver, 2011.

Figure 11 (right): Corinthian order by Sterling Doster, 2005.

The Birth of the Grand Tour:
TOPOGRAPHICAL SKETCHES AND DESCRIPTIONS
FROM SEVENTEENTH-CENTURY ROME BY CLAUDE LORRAIN
AND RICHARD LASSELS

The Voyage of Italy *by the Yorkshire-born Catholic priest, Richard Lassels (c.1603-1668), has been described as "the most influential English guidebook of the period."* [1] *Written during the 1650s and 1660s, its emphasis on art and architecture profoundly shaped the development of the "Grand Tour," an expression coined by Lassels to describe the educational trip to Italy that became almost obligatory for British architects, artists, and aristocrats during the following century. The transcribed excerpts presented here, including descriptions of the Colosseum, the Forum, and St. Peter's complement a selection of Roman topographical drawings by Claude Lorrain (c. 1604-82), Lassels' contemporary and the greatest of the ideal landscape painters. Although Claude's preparatory studies for paintings and the* liber veritatis *series of drawings he made to record his completed canvases have been widely published, the sketches of Roman buildings and landscapes shown here, almost certainly made for the purposes of personal study, are little known and in most cases have never been exhibited.* [2] *These drawings are remarkable for the evident mastery of a range of media and techniques— chalk, graphite, white gouache, brushed washes, and pen and ink—and for their enduring evocative power as observed by Henry James: "Claude must have haunted the very places of one's personal preference and adjusted their divine undulations to his splendid scheme of romance, his view of the poetry of life. He was familiar with aspects in which there wasn't a single uncompromising line. I saw a few days ago a small finished sketch from his hand, in the possession of an American artist, which was almost startling in its clear reflection of forms unaltered by the two centuries that have dimmed and cracked the paint and canvas."* [3] *–RTJ*

THE COLOSSEUM AND ARCH
OF CONSTANTINE [4]

Descending from hence I went to the old amphitheater, called now the Coliseo, because of a colossean statue that stood in it. [5] This is one of the rarest pieces of antiquity in Rome, and though Rome be grown again by her new pallaces [into] one of the finest cities of Europe, yet her very ruines are finer than her new buildings. And though I am not ignorant how Rome, since her Ladyship governed the world and was at her greatness, hath been six several times ruined and sacked by the envy and avarice of barbarous nations…whose malice was so great against Rome that of thirty-six triumphal arches once in Rome, there remain but four now visibly appearing; that of ten *Thermae* [baths] anciently, but two remain any way visible; that of seven Circos, but one now appears. Yet as of fair ladies there remain even in their old age fair rests of comliness, so the very ruines of Rome, which malice could not reach to nor avarice carry away, are yet so comely that they ravish still the beholders eye with their beauties, and make good the saying of an ancient author that *Roma jacens quoque miraculo est:* "Rome is a miracle even in its ruines." But to return to the Coliseo, it's another wonder of the world and I wonder indeed how such prodigious stones could either be laid together in a building, or being laid together, could fall. Vespasian began it but Domitian finished it, and Martial flattered it as a wonder which outstript all the wonders of Egypt and its pyramids. It was of a prodigious height, as that part of it yet standing sheweth. The form of it was round without and oval within, and the outside of it was adorned with the three orders of pillars; great arches below, open galleries above, both to walk in and to let people into the amphitheater and out again without crowding, so that two hundred thousand people could go in or out in half an hours time without crowding. Within it went up from below by steps of stone unto the top, and afforded room enough to all that world of people to sit conveniently and see the combats and sports that were exhibited in the arena. Anciently the top of it was set round with statues, and in time of great heats or rains it was all overspred with great sails.[6] From its roundish form it got the name of amphitheater from seeing on all sides. Underneath were the caves for the wild beasts, out of which they turned them loose to fight, sometimes against condemned men, sometimes against innocent Christians. Nero made the Christians be clad in the skins of beasts and so to be exposed to lyons and bears. Sometimes also gladiators fought against gladiators, and one gladiator against twenty others; nay the very noble Romans themselves would now and then fight here publickly, either to shew sport or valour. And all this was done by the politick Romans to teach men not to be afraid of bloodshed and death in time of wars, with which they had been so acquainted in time of peace.

The old round rubbage of brick which is here near the amphitheater was anciently a fine fountain called Meta Sudans, serving for the use of those that came to the sports here. It was all faced with marble and had a statue of Jupiter of brass upon it.[7]

Hard by stands the triumphal arch of Constantin the Great. It's all of marble, with a world of curious statues anciently, but now headless, and with histories in *bassi rilievi* [low relief]. It was erected to him in memory of his victory over the tyrant Maxentius, as to the freer of the city and founder of publick quiet, as the words here import: *Libertatori Urbis, Fundatori Quietis.*

THE FORUM ROMANUM[8]

From hence I entered into the *Campo Vaccino* [Forum Romanum] and presently fell upon three pillars of admirable structure: they belonged to the temple of Jupiter Stator built by Romulus.[9] The occasion was this: Romulus in a battle against the Sabins, seeing his men give back, made a vow presently to Jupiter that if he would stop their flight and make them stand to it, he would build him a temple: *Siste foedam fugam* [Stay their shameful flight], said he to Jupiter.[10] The men stood and the temple was built to Jupiter Stator, who made men stand. But this Jupiter Stator could not make his own temple stand for it's now so ruined that antiquaries are scarce sure where it stood.

Close to these three pillars stands the church of Santa Maria Liberatrice at the foot of the Palatin hill. Why this church is so called, both a long writing in the church, and Baronius in his annals, tell at length. Near to this church stood the Lacus Curtii, a stinking puddle which annoi'd the Romans much and which the oracle assured was not to be stopt up but by casting into it the most pretious thing in Rome.[11]

Figure 1 (opposite): Claude Lorrain, *Self-portrait,* Pen and brown ink and brown wash, heightened with white, over black chalk, on blue paper. © Trustees of the British Museum.

Figure 2 (top right): Claude Lorrain, *Interior, Colosseum, Rome,* 1635-40, 170 mm x 118 mm, Brush drawing in brown wash. © Trustees of the British Museum.

Figure 3 (right): Claude Lorrain, *Arch of Constantine and Colosseum, Rome,* 1635-40, 152 mm x 94 mm, Pen and brown ink. © Trustees of the British Museum.

Hereupon the ladies threw in their best jewels and the noblemen, every one, what he had the most pretious, but all in vain. At last Curtius, a brave young nobleman, thinking that there was nothing more pleasant than a gallant man, mounting on horseback in a brave equipage, in sight of all the people, jumpt into this lake alive, as a victime devoted to his countries service and the hole hereupon closed. I confess a brave cavalier is a pretious jewel indeed, and I remember that a Roman lady having shewed her jewels to Cornelia, the mother of the Gracchi, and having desired her to shew also her jewels, she called for her two young sons (brave youths) and said: "Here, Madam, are my jewels."[12] And in my opinion, Curtius was somewhat vainglorious to think himself to be the bravest man in the city; if the votes and judgment of all the people had declared him to be so (as they did afterwards declare Scipio Nasica to be the best man of all the Romans, and the matrons declared Sulpitia to be the chastest matron of her time[13]) then he might have devoted himself more freely for his country's safety.

Going on from hence on the right hand still, I came to the door of the Farnese's garden. This garden stands upon the mount Palatin where anciently the Emperors had their pallace which took up all the upper part of this hill, but not all the skirts of it; for I find that the goddess Feaver and the goddess Viriplaca had their temples here, and Catalin and Cicero their houses. Entring into this garden I found some pretty

waterworks and grottes at the entrance, and fine high walks above, overlooking the place where the Circus Maximus stood anciently. The scholars of the English Colledge in Rome have a piece of this hill for their vines and recreation place, to breath on upon dayes of vacancy.

Following still my right hand, I came to the Arch of Titus, a triumphal arch erected to him upon his victory over the Jews. Hence you see here engraven in *mezzo rilievo* [mid relief] the said emperor in a triumphant chariot, and, on the other, the holy candlestick of the Temple of Hierusalem, the ark of the alliance, and the tables of the Law, which this emperour brought with him after his taking of Hierusalem, to grace his triumph. This is the most ancient triumphal arch in Rome and it stood in the via Sacra which went under it.

Wheeling about the Campo Vaccino, still on my right hand, I came to the church of Sancta Francesca Romana, otherwise called Santa Maria Nuova. Here I saw the neat tombe of that saint in brass guilt, made at the cost of Pope Innocent the X. Here's also cut in white marble, and standing upon an altar, the history of the Popes returning again to Rome from Avignon. I saw also here a rare sute of hangings belonging to this church and given by the sister of Pope Innocent the X.[14]

Hard by stands the Temple of Peace, that is, some remnants of that temple.[15] It was once the most of all the temples (as the pillar before

St. Mary Majors great door which belonged to this temple sheweth).[16] It was 200 foot large and 300 long, but no little signes of its beauty remain, warres and time defacing the monuments of peace. It was built by Vespasian who placed in it the spoiles of the Temple of Hierusalem brought to Rome by Titus. Behind this temple stands a neat garden belonging once to Cardinal Pio, where I saw neat water works. It's now sold to another master.

Going on still in the *Campo Vaccino* on the right hand, I came to the round church of St. Cosmo and St. Damiano, anciently the temple of Castor and Pollux because the Romans having seen two men upon sweating horses that told the news of a battle wonn by their consul and so vanished they imagined them to be Castor and Pollux and thereupon decreed them this temple.[17] The mosaick work in the roof of the tribune deserves your particular attention for the symbolical figures sake.

Going on still, I came to the church of St. Lorenzo in Miranda. It was once a temple dedicated to Fasutina the emperess by her husband Antoninus. Poor man! He could not make her an honest woman in her lifetime and yet he would needs make her a goddess after her death. The porch of this church is stately still by reason of its great marble pillars.

THE PANTHEON[18]

From hence I went to the Rotonda otherwise called anciently the Pantheon because it was dedicated to all the gods. This is a bolder piece of architecture than men think. For whereas other vaults are strengthened and made good by being shut up close at the top and in the center of the vault, which hinders the vault from shrinking, here this great massive vault is left wide open at the top, with a hole above three yards wide in diameter. Indeed Sebastianus Serlius, an experienced man in frabriks, thinks this church to be the unick example of perfect architecture, and Pliny, in his time, placed it among the rarest works that were then extant. It had no window in it, nor any other light, but what comes in at the wide hole mentioned above. Anciently it was covered with brazen tiles and those guilt too, as Lipsius thinks, but now it's covered with great flatt stones. It's a hundred and forty foot high and as many broad, and yet it hath no pillars to bear up that great roof. Indeed it hath thrust all the pillars out of doors, and makes them wait in the porch where there are thirteen great pillars all of one piece, each one 53 foot high and six indiameter all of a granite or speckled marble.[19] The *capitelli* [capitals] of these pillars are the best in Rome of Corinthian order. Here is the tomb of the incomparable painter Raphael Urbino. [...]

This temple and its porch were so lined anciently with brass that there was enough of it to make divers great canons by Pope Urban's command and the great canopy with the four pillars which adorn St. Peter's High Altar.[20] And though the people and Pasquin, two equally senseless things, murmured much at the taking away of this brass, yet seeing the Pantheon received no damage thereby, and seeing it was improved to that height that it became *Ecclesiae ornamentum et urbi munimentum* ["ornament of the church and safeguard of the city"], the wiser sort of men thought it well employed, and let the people and malice talk. I had almost forgot to tell you that this temple was made by Agrippa, who had been thrice consul as the words in the architrave of the porch yet shew.[21]

Figure 4 (opposite): Claude Lorrain, *Ponte Molle, Rome,* c. 1660, 178 mm x 105 mm, Pen and brown ink, with brown and gray wash. © Trustees of the British Museum.

Figure 5 (above): Claude Lorrain, *Temple of Castor and Pollux, Forum Romanum, Rome,* 1640-45, 176 mm x 113 mm, Black chalk, touched with gray-brown wash. © Trustees of the British Museum.

THE PIAZZA, FAÇADE, AND INTERIOR OF ST. PETER'S[22]

Presently after, you come to the Piazza of St. Peter, built round about with a noble portico of freestone born up by four rowes of stately round pillars, under which not only the procession upon Corpus Christi day marcheth in the shade, but also all people may go dry and out of the sun in summer or winter unto St. Peters Church or the Vatican Pallace. This portico is built in an oval form and fetcheth in the great piazza which is before St. Peters Church and therefore can be no less than half a mile in compass. This noble structure was begun by Alexander the VII and half of it finished, and the other half is now almost finished.[23] I never saw any thing more stately than this. The number of the pillars and of the statues on the top I do not justly remember. In the midst of this piazza stands the famous *guglia* [obelisk]; which was brought out of Aegypt in the time of the old Romans, and dedicated to Augustus Caesar and Tiberius, as the words upon it import. It lay hid long in Nero's circus, which was there where now St. Peter's sacristy is, and at last Sixtus Quintus having proposed great reward to him that would venture to set it up here without breaking, it was happily undertaken by Dominico Fontana, a rare architect of Como, and so placed as you see it now. The manner of bringing it out of Aegypt and of erecting it here are both painted in fresco upon the walls of the Vatican library: This *guglia* is all of one stone except the basis and it hath no hieroglyphes upon it. The stone is a granite, or speckled marble, which together with its basis, is a hundred and eight foot high. It rests upon four lyons of brass guilt and at the top of it is planted a cross of brass mounted upon three mountains with a star over them (the arms of Sixtus Quintus whose name was Montalto.) Within the cross is a piece of the Holy Cross of our Saviour, included here by Sixtus Quintus. The whole *guglia* is said to weigh 956,148 pound weight. I wonder what scales they had to weigh it with.

On each side of this *guglia* is to stand fair fountains, one whereof is that which is seen there now, which throweth up such a quantity of water that it maketh a mist alwaies about it, and oftentimes a rainbow when the sun strikes obliquely upon it. This Piazza is capable of two hundred thousand men, and delivers you up to the stairs which lead you up to the church of St. Peter.

Coming therefore near to St. Peter's Church, I was glad to see that noble structure, where greatness and neatness, bulk and beauty, are so mingled together that it's neither neat only, like a spruce gallery, nor vast only, like a great hall; but it's rather like a proper man and yet well proportioned. You mount up to this church by an easie ascent of four and twenty steps of marble stairs, as long as the frontispice of the church is wide; these stairs were those of the old church of St. Peter, and Baronius observes that when the Emperor Charlemagne mounted up those stairs first, he kissed every step as he went up.

These stairs lead you up to the frontispice of the church, which hath five dores in it letting you into the porch; and these dores are cheeked with vast round pillars of freestone 24 foot in compass, and eighty-six in heighth. Over these pillars runs the architrave, and over it the lodge [loggia] or great balcone, where the Pope is crowned, and where he gives his benediction upon Easter day. Over this lodge

runs a continual baluster or row of rails, upon which stand thirteen vast statues of our Saviour and his apostles cut in stone.

Entring into the porch, you will admire the length, breadth, and height of it. For the length of it, it's two hundred eighty-nine foot; the breadth, forty-four foot; the height, a hundred thirty-three foot. It's adorned on both sides with great marble pillars and a curious guilt roofe. In fine, this porch any where else would be a handsome church.

Over against the five doors of this porch, stand the five doors of the church, one whereof is called the Porta Sancta, and only open in the Jubily year, the others are dayly open; and the two principal doors are called *Valvae Sancti Petri* [doors of St. Peter], and covered with brass by the command of Eugenius the IV whose memorable actions, to wit the crowning of the Emperor Sigismond and the reunion of the Greek Church with the Latin, are expressed in them. These *Valvae* are thirteen foot wide and forty-five high; and to them all pope's bulls are nailed at their publication.

Entring into the church, I found it to be built in cross wise containing in length five hundred and twenty foot, and three hundred eighty-five in breadth. So that it passeth in greatness the famous temples of antiquity, to wit: Solomon's Temple, long threescore cubits; the Temple of Diana in Ephesus, long four hundred twenty-five foot; and the great Moski at Fez, long a hundred and fifty cubits.

The roof or vault of this church is arched with great squares and each square is adorned with a great guilt rose, which almost fills the square. This roof is born up by great pillars of freestone of a square form, whose *capitelli* are curiously wrought after the Corinthian order, and joined to one another above by arches and a perpetual cornice, over which are cut in stone the statues of several moral virtues. These pillars are a hundred and five foot in compasse, and distant forty foot one from another. On that side of them which looks towards the body of the church; they are to be overcrusted with white marble, with two rows of niches in them for great statues of brass guilt. The other sides of these pillars are already adorned with a neat overcrusting of a reddish marble beset with the heads of the primitive martyred popes, held up by two angels, and with the pigeon of Innocent the X (who made this decoration) and all these are in *mezzo rilievo* [mid relief], and of pure white alabaster. Behind these pillars is a large ile or passage, and behind that ile immediately stand fair chappels, which flanck up this church notably, and each chappel is graced with a little cupola of its own.

In the midst of the cross building of this church is mounted the great cupola, which looks like a great crown wherewith this Queen of churches is crowned. It rests upon four *Pilastri* or great pillars which make the corners of the cross of this church, and from them it riseth into such a high vault, that it seems to walk into Heaven. It's full as round as the Pantheon in Rome, that is, it carrieth the compass of an hundred and seventy paces, as you may easily measure upon the circle of white marble in the pavement which environeth the Altar of St. Peter, and is made there on purpose perpendicularly under the cupola to shew its greatness. The inside of this cupola is curiously painted with pictures in mosaick work representing a Heaven: indeed nothing but Heaven itself can be finer or higher. So that I may say truly to Rome with Rutillius, *Non procul a caelo per tua Templa sumus* ["on account of your temples we are not far from Heaven"].[24]

In a word this cupola is the boldest piece of architecture that perhaps the world hath seen and it was the last and greatest work of Sixtus Quintus [and] his purse.

The four *pilastri* upon which this cupola resteth are vast square pillars, a hundred and twenty foot in compass, and capable of stairs within them and large sacristyes above for the holy relicks that are kept in them, to wit: the Volto Santo or print of our Saviours face, which he imprinted in the handkercher of St. Veronici; the piece of the Holy Cross; the top of the lance wherewith our Saviours side was pierced; and the head of St. Andrew the Apostle translated hither into his brother's church by Pius Secundus.

THE DOME OF ST. PETER'S[25]

Having thus seen this church both within and underground, I was desirous to see it also above. Ascending therefore by a fair staircase I arrived at the great terrass over the lodge, and there saw the thirteen statutes of our Saviour and the twelve apostles near hand, which seem below little taller than the statue of our tallest men and yet here above are eighteen foot high. There also I saw the several little cupolas, which give light to the side chappels of this church, and look like the issue and spawn of the Great Cupola. Then, mounting a little higher, I beheld a

Figure 6 (above): Claude Lorrain, *St. Peter's, Rome* (showing one of Bernini's short-lived bell towers), c. 1640-41, 307 mm x 211 mm, Black chalk. © Trustees of the British Museum.

Figure 7 (right): Claude Lorrain, *Interior of St. Peter's, Rome,* c. 1640-45, 219 mm x 160 mm, Black chalk. © Trustees of the British Museum.

rare fabrick of the mother cupola, both within and without: the staires to mount up into it; the double vault in it and stairs between the two vaults; the lantern upon the Cupola; the narrow stairs in one of the pillars of that lantern up to the ball; lastly, the straight neck of the passage into the ball and the ball itself are all worth particular observation as being the height of architecture. The ball itself of brass guilt is capable of thirty men, though from below it lookes only as big as twice a man's head. We were eight in it at once and I am sure we could have placed thrice as many more. Upon the round ball is mounted a great Cross of iron guilt to signifie that the vertue of the Cross by our Saviours passion hath triumped over the world of which this round Ball is the express emblem. From this cupola we had a perfect veiw of Rome under us and of all the villas about it. But nothing was so wonderful as to see St. Peters church and palace look like a town under us, which we knew to be but one church and house.

You will wonder perchance too when you shall hear that this church is the eighth wonder of the world, that the pyramids of Egypt, the walls of Babylon, the Pharos, Colossus, etc., were but heaps of stones compared to this fabrick; that it hath put all antiquity to the blush, and all posterity to a non plus; that its several parts are all incomparable masterpieces, its pictures all originals, its statues perfect models; that

it hath a revenue of above twenty thousand pounds a year onely for the fabrick; that it hath cost till the year 1654 (the accounts being then summed up) forty millions of crownes; that most of the popes since Julius the II (and they have been twenty-three in all) have heartened and advanced this work; that the prime architects of the world, Sangalla, Bramante, Baldassere [Peruzzi], [Michelangelo] Buonarota, Giacomo della Porta, Giovani Fontana, Carlo Maderno, and now Cavaliero Bernino,[26] have brought it on to this perfection; that the whole church itself is nothing but the quintessence of wit and wealth strained into a religious design of making a handsome house to God and of fulfilling the divine oracle which promised that *magna erit gloria domus istius novissimae plusquam primae* [Haggai, 2.10: "The glory of this latter house shall be greater than of the former"]. ❦

Figure 8 (opposite): Claude Lorrain, *Ripa Grande, Rome,* c. 1638, 175 mm x 114 mm, Pen and brown ink, brown wash. © Trustees of the British Museum.

Figure 9 (left): Claude Lorrain, *Arch of Constantine, Rome,* c. 1645-50, 249 mm x 188 mm, Pen and brown ink, brown and gray wash. © Trustees of the British Museum.

NOTES

1 Edward Chaney, "Lassels, Richard (c.1603–1668)," *Oxford Dictionary of National Biography* (Oxford: Oxford University Press, 2004); see also Edward Chaney, *The Evolution of the Grand Tour Anglo-Italian Cultural Relations since the Renaissance* (London and New York: Routledge, 2000).

2 For a recent account and complete bibliography of Claude's drawings see Richard Rand, *Claude Lorrain—The Painter as Draftsman* (New Haven and London: Yale University Press, 2006).

3 Henry James, *Italian Hours* (Boston and New York: Houghton Mifflin Company, 1909) p. 233.

4 Richard Lassels, *The Voyage of Italy: Or a Compleat Journey through Italy.* Vol. II (Paris: Vincent du Moutier, 1670), pp. 119-123 (hereafter Lassels, *Voyage*). In these excerpts Lassels' original orthography has mostly been retained, including different spellings for the same words in some cases; for the ease of reading, however, punctuation has been modernized and typographical errors have been corrected. It is hoped that sufficient of the period character of the prose has been retained to help transport the reader to seventeenth-century Rome.

5 The Colossus was originally a giant bronze portrait of Nero by Zenodorus which was altered by Vespasian to represent Sol.

6 The velarium.

7 The Meta Sudans was built by Domitian and took its name from its similarity to the turning posts in the circus. The remains of its concrete core were removed in 1936. See Brenda Longfellow, "Reflections of Imperialism: the Meta Sudans in Rome and the Provinces," *The Art Bulletin*, 92 (2010) pp. 275-292.

8 Lassels, *Voyage*, pp. 128-134.

9 These three columns in fact belong to the Temple of Castor (Aedes Castoris) as rebuilt in the Augustan period.

10 Livy, I, xii, 5.

11 Livy, VII, vi, 1-6.

12 Valerius Maximus, IV, 4.

13 Martial, X, 35, 38.

14 Presumably Olimpia Maidalchini, known as Donna Olimpia, the influential sister-in-law of Innocent X.

15 Actually the Basilica Nova, which was begun by Maxentius and completed by Constantine.

16 This column was removed from the Basilica Nova in 1614 by Paul V to be erected, with an different capital, in front of Santa Maria Maggiore.

17 The church of SS. Cosma e Damiano in fact comprises two ancient buildings: the circular Temple of Romulus, erected by Maxentius to his divinized son, and one of the flanking halls of Vespasian's Temple of Peace.

18 Lassels, *Voyage*, pp. 235-238.

19 Of the sixteen monolithic columns in the pronaos of the Pantheon, the three easternmost of these are seventeenth-century replacements and perhaps explain Lassels' arithmetic.

20 The baldacchino by Bernini and Borromini; Urban VIII's removal of the bronze girders from the porch roof resulted in the pasquinade: *Quod non fecerunt barbari, fecerunt Barberini* ["What the barbarians did not do, the Barberini did"].

21 Studies of brickstamps used in the Pantheon prove that the architrave inscription refers not to the current building which is Hadrianic in date but to its Agrippan predecessor.

22 Lassels, *Voyage*, pp. 26-34.

23 The architect of the piazza was Gianlorenzo Bernini.

24 Rutilius Namatianus, *De Reditu Suo*, I, 50.

25 Lassels, *Voyage*, pp. 45-8.

26 In another passage, when discussing the obelisk in the Piazza Navona, Lassels notes that Bernini had briefly fallen from papal favor as a result of the debacle over the bell towers: "Thanks to that ingenious architect Cavalier Bernini who set it [the obelisk] up there in the Anno Sancto, and whom it set up too again in the Popes favour, Innocent the X, which he had lost by a crack in the roof of the porch of St. Peter's church caused by the heavy steeple which he had placed up on it.", Lassels, *Voyage*, p. 97. On the bell towers see Sarah McPhee, *Bernini and the Bell Towers: Architecture and Politics at the Vatican* (New Haven: Yale University Press, 2002); for a rare depiction of the South bell tower during its short-lived existence see the Claude sketch above.

Administration
and Sponsors

SPONSORS

The publication of *The Classicist No. 10* has been made possible thanks to the generous contributions of the following:

Karen LaGatta

———

E. R. Butler & Co.

———

Jamb.
Fairfax & Sammons Architecture

———

Balmer Architectural Mouldings
Chadsworth's 1-800-COLUMNS
Chesney's
Curtis & Windham Architects, LLC
Doyle Herman Design Associates
Dyad Communications, Inc.
Eric J. Smith Architect, PC
Ferguson & Shamamian Architects, LLP
Flower Construction
Foster Reeve & Associates, Inc.
G. P. Schafer Architect, PLLC
Gold Coast Metal Works, Inc.
Gregory Lombardi Design
Harrison Design Associates – Atlanta Office
Historical Arts & Castings, Inc.
Hyde Park Mouldings
The I. Grace Company
Ike Kligerman Barkley Architects
John B. Murray Architect, LLC
John Milner Architects
Ken Tate Architect, P.A.
Kuiken Brothers Company, Inc.
Leonard Porter Studio, LLC
Mark P. Finlay Architects, AIA
McKinnon and Harris, Inc.
National Monuments Foundation
Oliver Cope Architect
Peter Pennoyer Architects
Peter Zimmerman Architects
Porphyrios Associates
R. D. Rice Construction
Reilly Windows & Doors
Robert A. M. Stern Architects, LLP
Vella Interiors
Waterworks
Zepsa Industries

———

Appleton & Associates, Inc.
Architectural Heritage
Carlisle Wide Plank Floors
David Ellison Architect
Lowe Hardware
University of Notre Dame
White River Hardwoods

———

Eberlein Design Consultants, Ltd
Griffiths Construction, Inc.
Historical Concepts
University of Miami School
of Architecture
Traditional Cut Stone
Historic Doors, LLC

———

Kais Custom Builders
Knight Architecture, LLC
Ralph L. Duesing, Architect, LLC

———

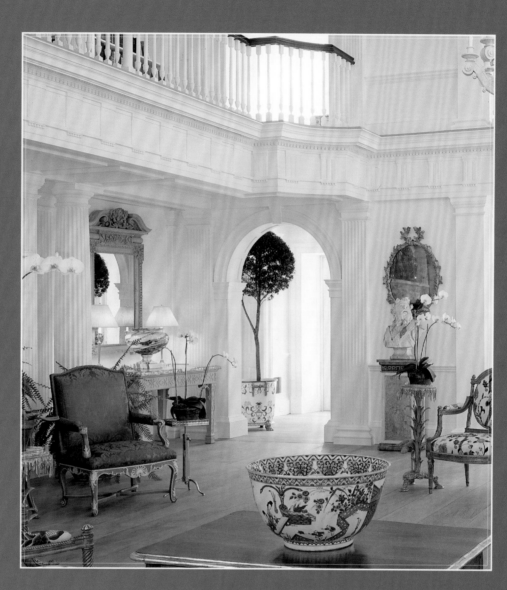

Balmer Architectural Mouldings Inc.

271 Yorkland Blvd. Toronto, ON, M2J 1S5 Canada
Tel: 416 491 6425 Fax: 416 491 7023
www.balmer.com

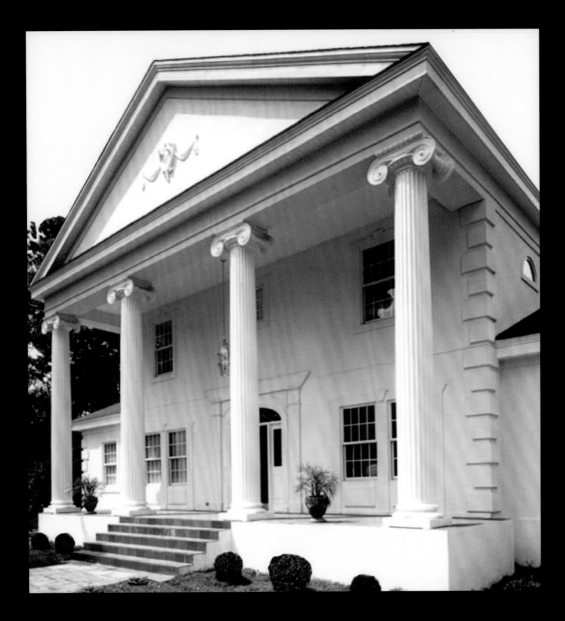

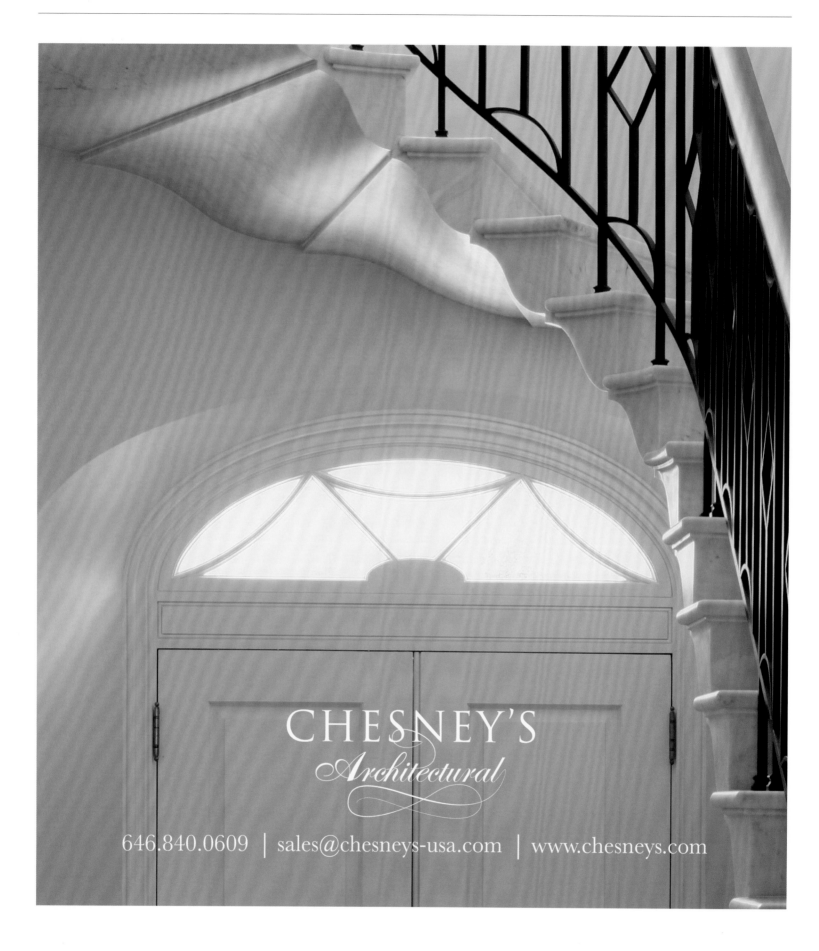

CURTIS & WINDHAM

Architects

INCORPORATED

WWW.CURTISANDWINDHAM.COM

Doyle Herman Design Associates
LANDSCAPE DESIGN

125 GREENWICH AVENUE | GREENWICH CT 06830 | PHONE 203 869 2900 | DHDA.COM

DYAD COMMUNICATIONS *design office*

IDENTITY, PRINT AND WEB / *dyadcom.com* / 215-636-0505

ERIC J. SMITH ARCHITECT
Professional Corporation

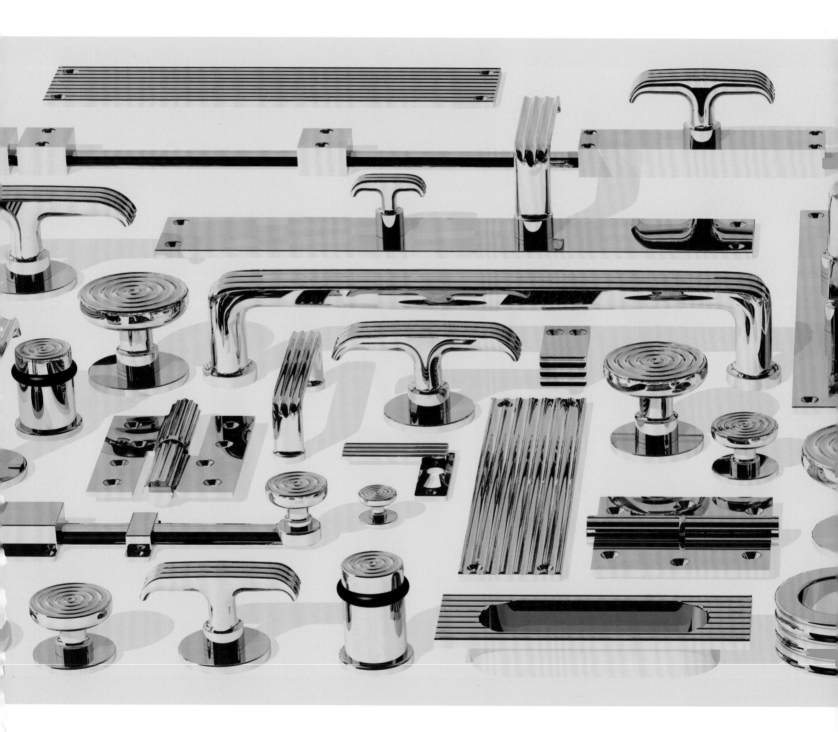

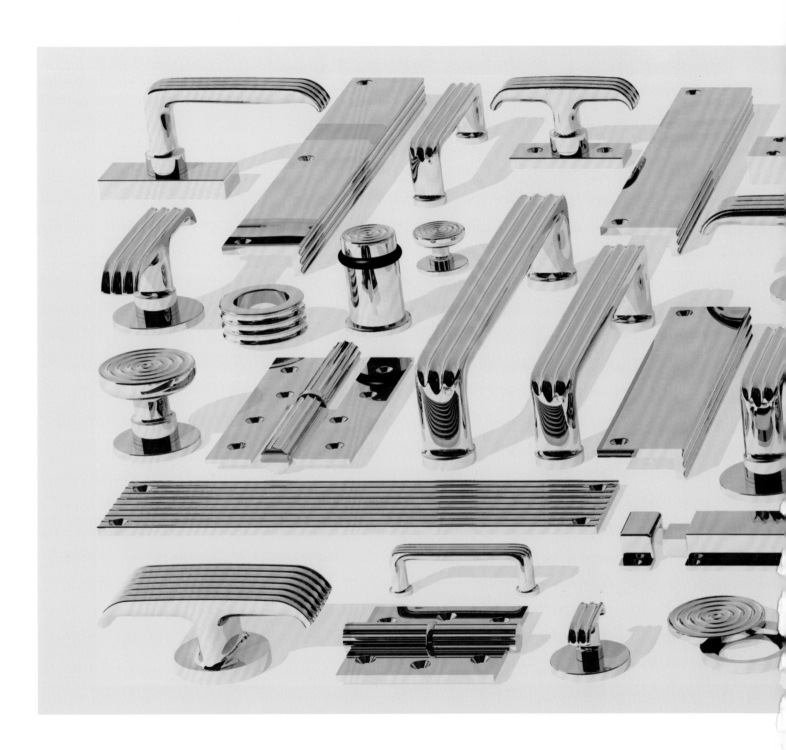

FLUTED DESIGN SERIES

G. BONOMI & FIGLI · E.R. BUTLER & CO.

Every door realizes a boundary between spaces; each represents a decision to be made. Knob, lever, turn or pull – the handle represents a primal point of connection and the possibility of discovery within. Since its inception, E.R. Butler & Co. has been committed to designing and producing the most exquisite architectural hardware with this unique understanding in mind. Respect for the traditions of craftsmanship and the artistry of historical eras meets a vibrant embrace of current technology and contemporary living in work renowned worldwide. The culmination of a matchless vision, their collections are shaped by rigorous research, distinctive design, uncompromising production values and personal service. The result is a compelling and enduring presence appropriate for every environment. With the launch of the Fluted Collection, G. Bonomi & Figli and E.R. Butler & Co. begin an exclusive partnership realizing shared values and a dedication to the progressive and powerful foresight of its founders. The revival of traditions begins with valuable insights from the past. In a stunning evocation of Modernism, the workshop in Tione di Trento produced prescient pieces of early twentieth century design in the International Style that comprised the origins of this sleek and sophisticated collection. This reconsideration of timeless beauty became the baseline not only for future collections but also for a fresh look at the possibilities of architectural hardware in the twenty-first century. Synthesizing efficiency in production and elegance of form, E.R. Butler & Co. has worked with the Bonomi family to introduce a revolutionary structure for design and manufacturing focused on consistency and compatibility. This hardware classification system embodies a holistic perspective on the needs of residential and commercial environments and provides the client with a guide that ensures a world of solutions for the range of technical and global applications. We are uniquely positioned with a collection and a comprehensive new approach to goods and services that proudly speaks to our heritage.

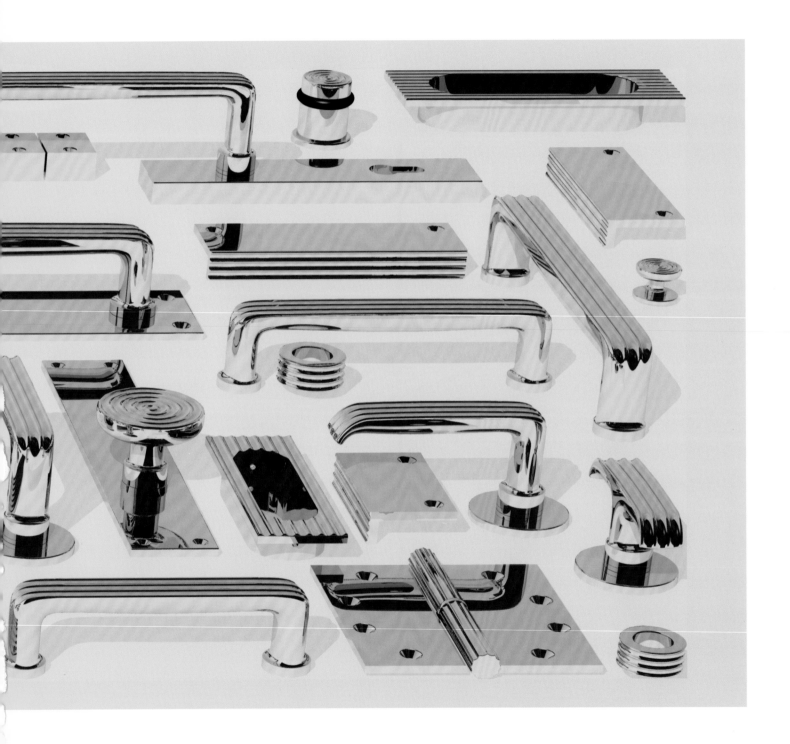

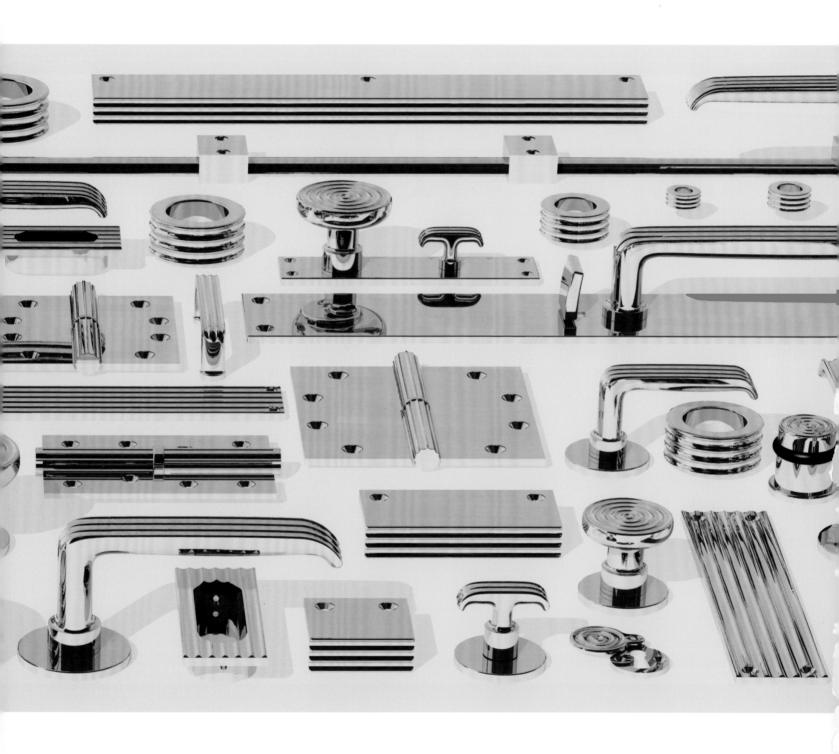

B̈

E. R. BUTLER & CO.

MANUFACTURERS

―――――――

WWW.ERBUTLER.COM

CATALOGUES AVAILABLE TO THE TRADE

SHOWROOMS BY APPOINTMENT

**FERGUSON &
SHAMAMIAN**
ARCHITECTS, LLP

270 LAFAYETTE STREET, NEW YORK, NY 10012
TELEPHONE: 212-941-8088 www.fergusonshamamian.com

PHOTOGRAPHY:DURSTON SAYLOR

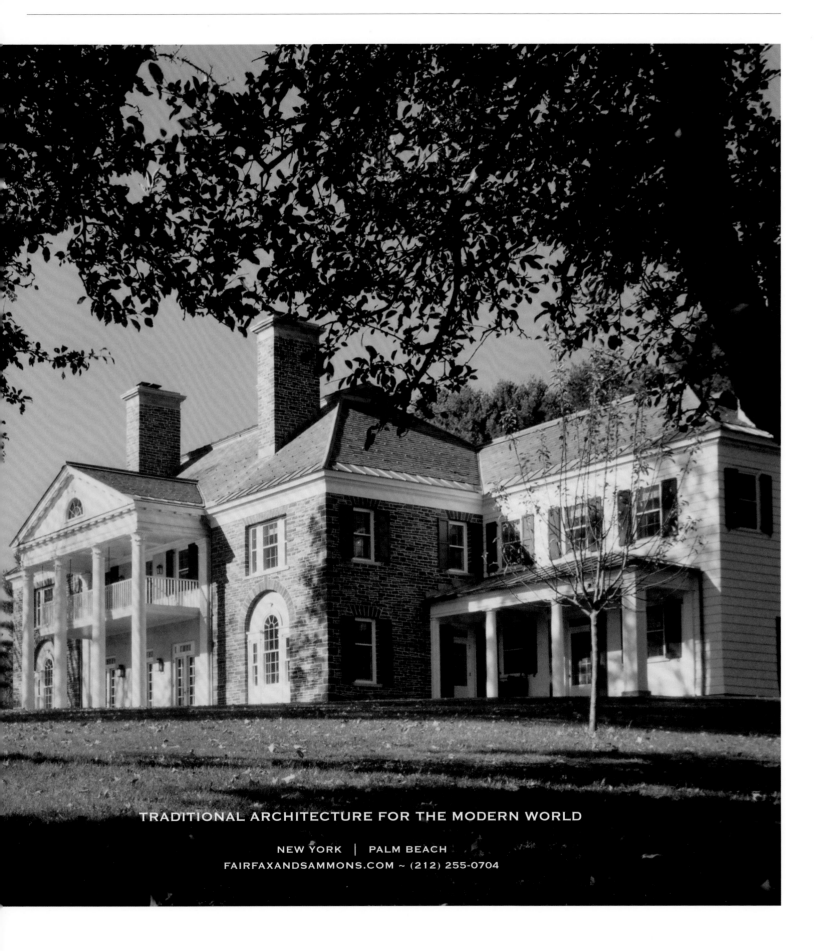

TRADITIONAL ARCHITECTURE FOR THE MODERN WORLD

NEW YORK | PALM BEACH
FAIRFAXANDSAMMONS.COM ~ (212) 255-0704

FLOWER CONSTRUCTION

FLOWCON.NET 973-543-5715

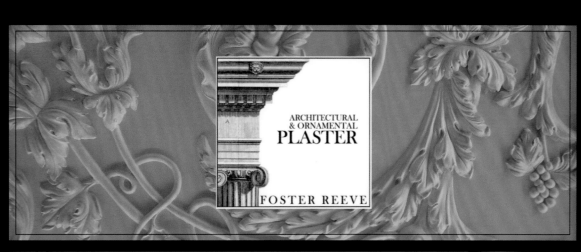

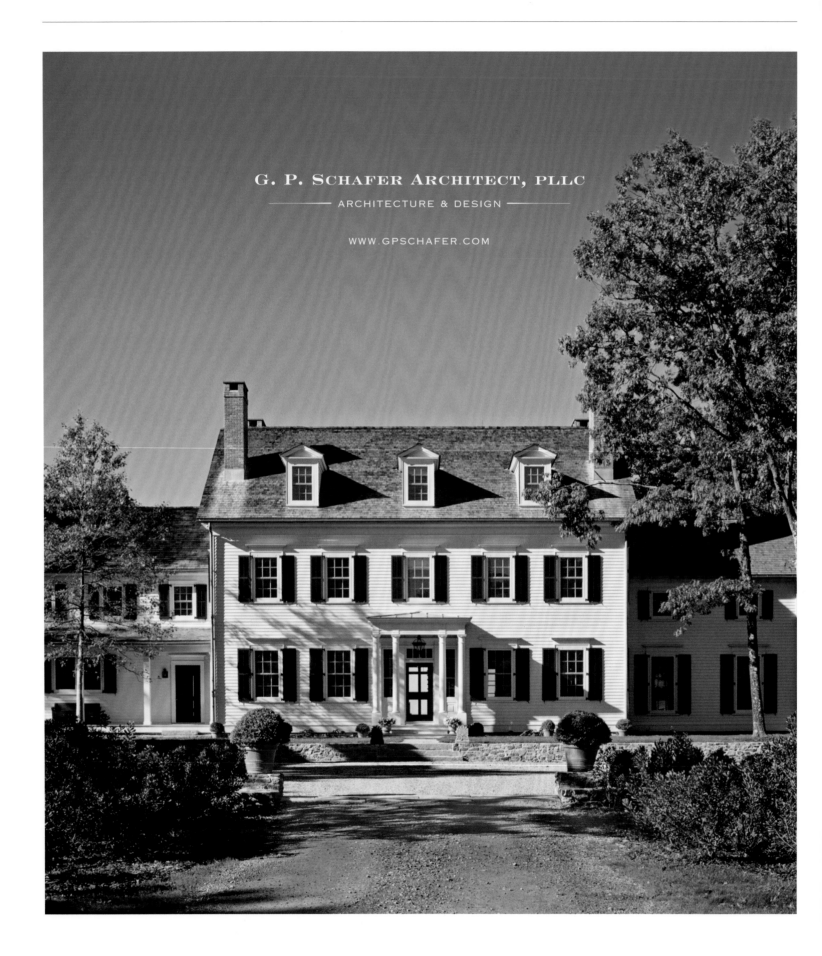

G. P. SCHAFER ARCHITECT, PLLC

—— ARCHITECTURE & DESIGN ——

WWW.GPSCHAFER.COM

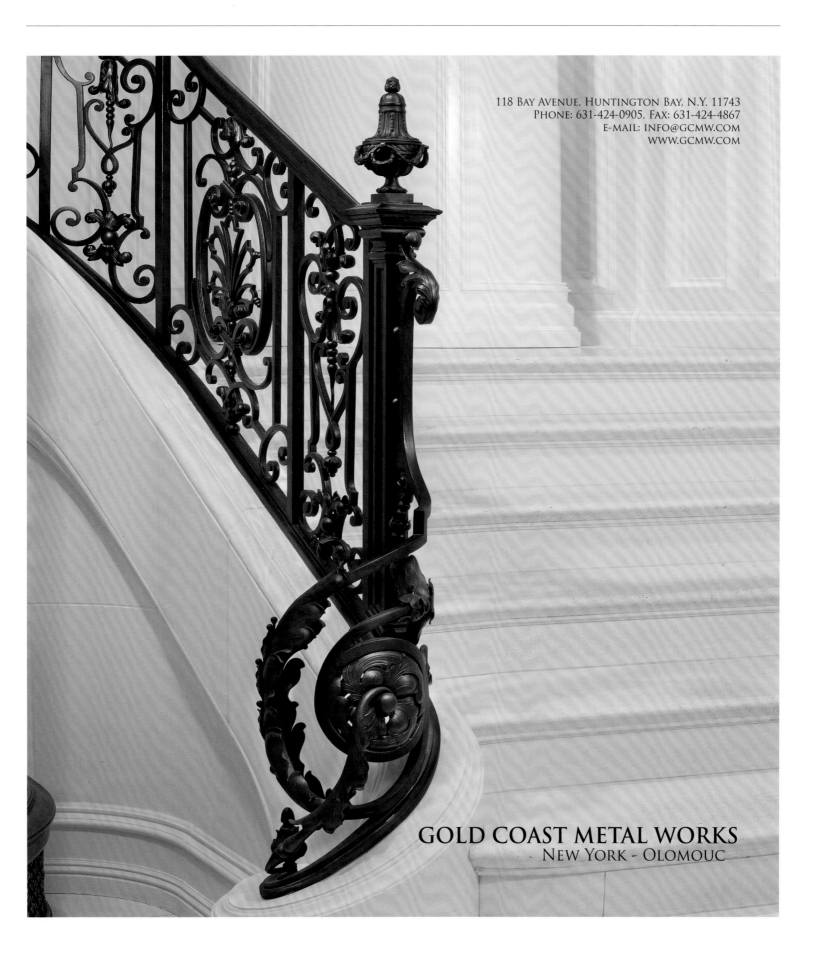

GOLD COAST METAL WORKS
New York - Olomouc

GREGORY LOMBARDI DESIGN
Landscape Architecture

Cambridge · Chatham · Palm Beach   617-492-2808   lombardidesign.com

HARRISON DESIGN ASSOCIATES
ARCHITECTURE & DESIGN

www.HarrisonDesignAssociates.com
866 688 3988

Atlanta | Beverly Hills | New York | St. Simons | Santa Barbara | Shanghai | Washington, DC

HISTORICAL ARTS & CASTINGS, INC.
www.historicalarts.com

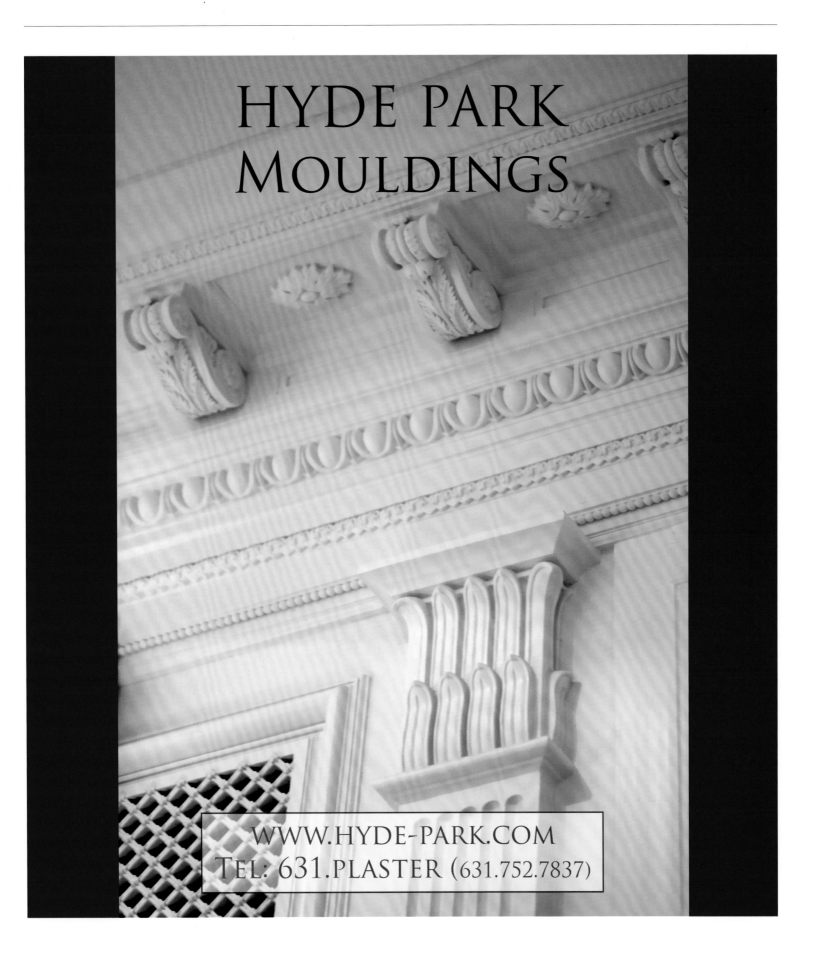

HYDE PARK
MOULDINGS

WWW.HYDE-PARK.COM
TEL: 631.PLASTER (631.752.7837)

We would like to congratulate

The Institute of

Classical Architecture and Art

for their 20 years

of dedication to preserving

the classical tradition

The

I·GRACE
COMPANY

Commissioned Private
Residences

www.igrace.com

IKE KLIGERMAN BARKLEY ARCHITECTS

NEW YORK • 212 268 0128
SAN FRANCISCO • 415 371 1850
WWW.IKBA.COM

Jamb.

97 Pimlico Road, London SW1W 8PH
T +44 (0) 20 7730 2122 www.jamb.co.uk

Traditionally hand-crafted lighting for
indoor and outdoor use

Jamb.

97 Pimlico Road, London SW1W 8PH
T +44 (0) 20 7730 2122 www.jamb.co.uk

Traditionally hand-crafted stone and marble
mantles, grates and accessories

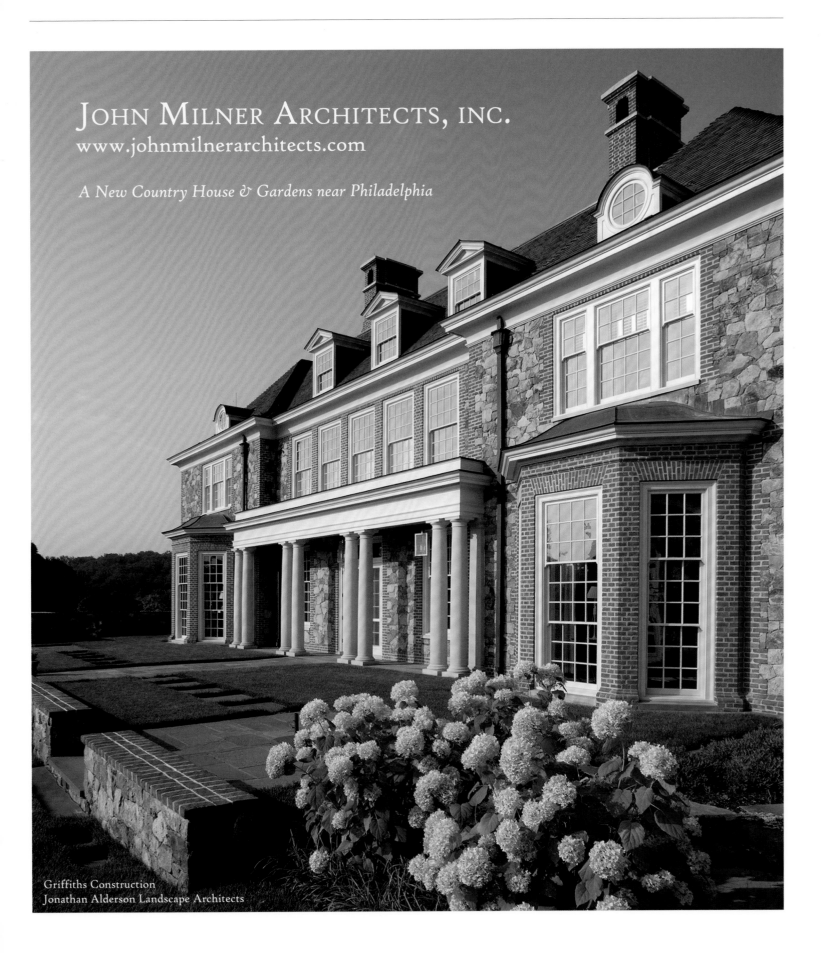

JOHN MILNER ARCHITECTS, INC.
www.johnmilnerarchitects.com

A New Country House & Gardens near Philadelphia

Griffiths Construction
Jonathan Alderson Landscape Architects

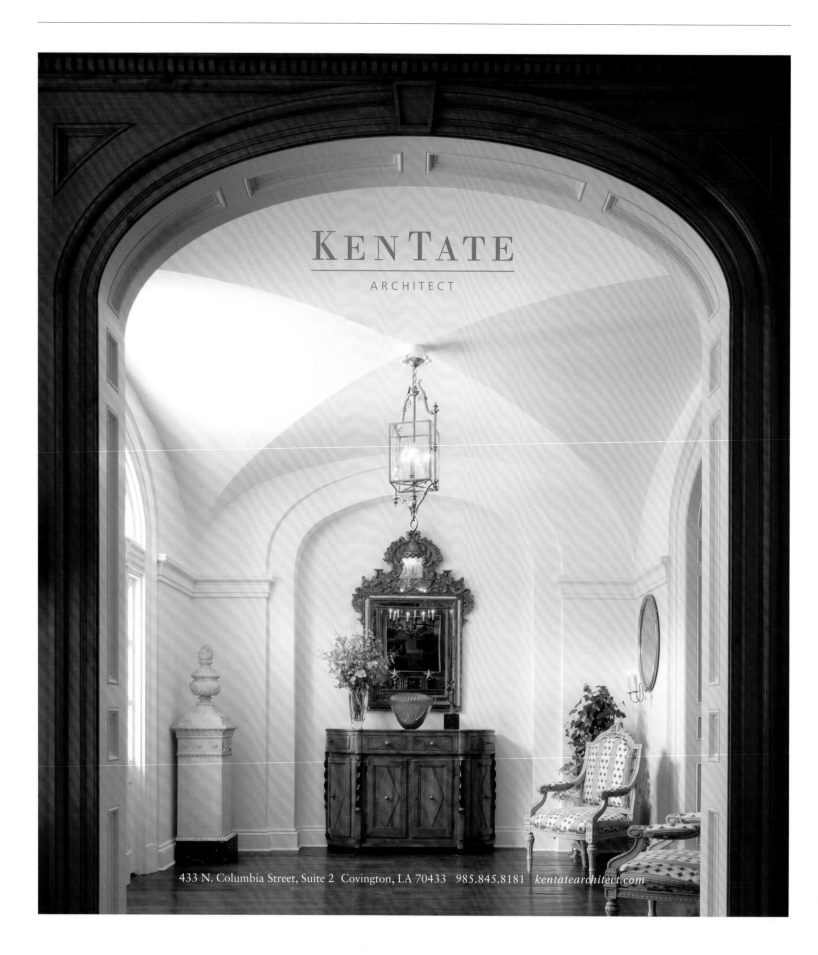

KEN TATE

ARCHITECT

433 N. Columbia Street, Suite 2 Covington, LA 70433   985.845.8181   *kentatearchitect.com*

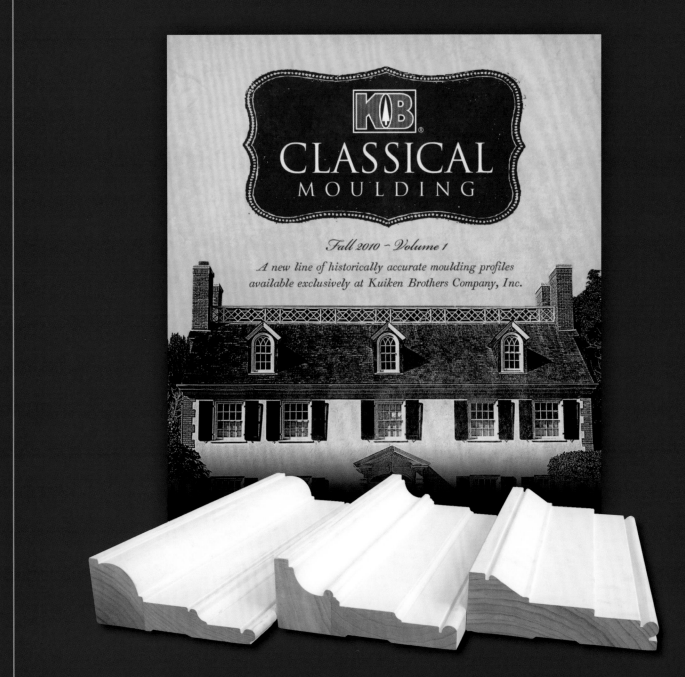

·LEONARD·PORTER·STVDIO·

PAINTINGS OF ANTIQVITY AND CLASSICAL MYTHOLOGY

WWW·LEONARDPORTER·COM

McKINNON AND HARRIS®
ESTATE · GARDEN · YACHT FURNITURE

SUBLIMIS · VIRTUS · SEMPITERNA

211 E. 59TH STREET · NEW YORK, NEW YORK 10022 · TO THE TRADE
212.371.8260 · www.mckinnonharris.com

NATIONAL MONUMENTS FOUNDATION
RODNEY MIMS COOK

EAST VIEW

RECONSTRUCTION OF THE OLMSTED DESIGNED

HISTORIC MIMS PARK

ATLANTA

WEST VIEW

AND INTRODUCING OUR NEW VIZERRA/VIMTREK 3-D VIRTUAL SMART TECHNOLOGY

Photography - Eric Piasecki

OLIVER COPE · ARCHITECT

151 WEST TWENTY-SIXTH STREET, NEW YORK, NEW YORK 10001

www.olivercope.com   *(212) 727-1225*

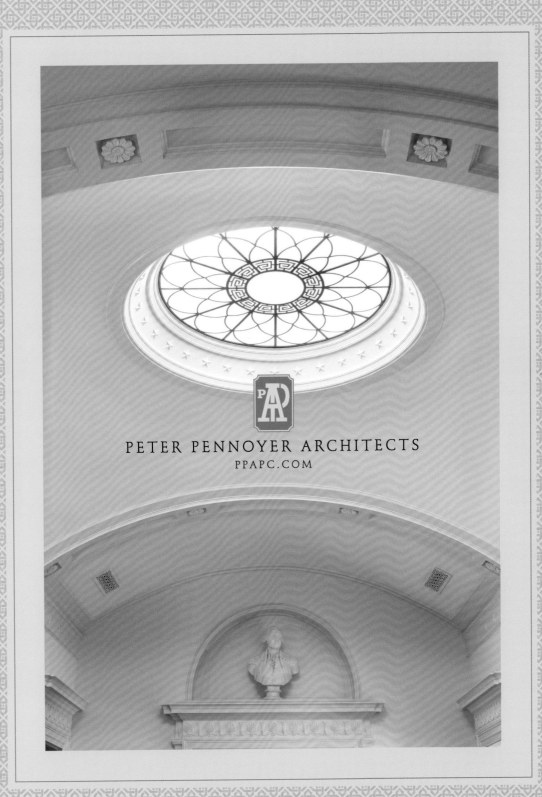

PETER PENNOYER ARCHITECTS
PPAPC.COM

Photography: Jonathan Wallen

Peter Zimmerman Architects

828 Old Lancaster Road Berwyn, Pennsylvania 19312
www.PZArchitects.com   (610) 647-6970

PORPHYRIOS
A S S O C I A T E S

Image shown: Duncan Aviation Galleries, Lincoln, NE © Porphyrios Associates   www.porphyrios.com

Architect:
Eric J. Smith

Builder:
Koral Bros. Inc.

REILLY
WINDOWS & DOORS

www.reillywd.com

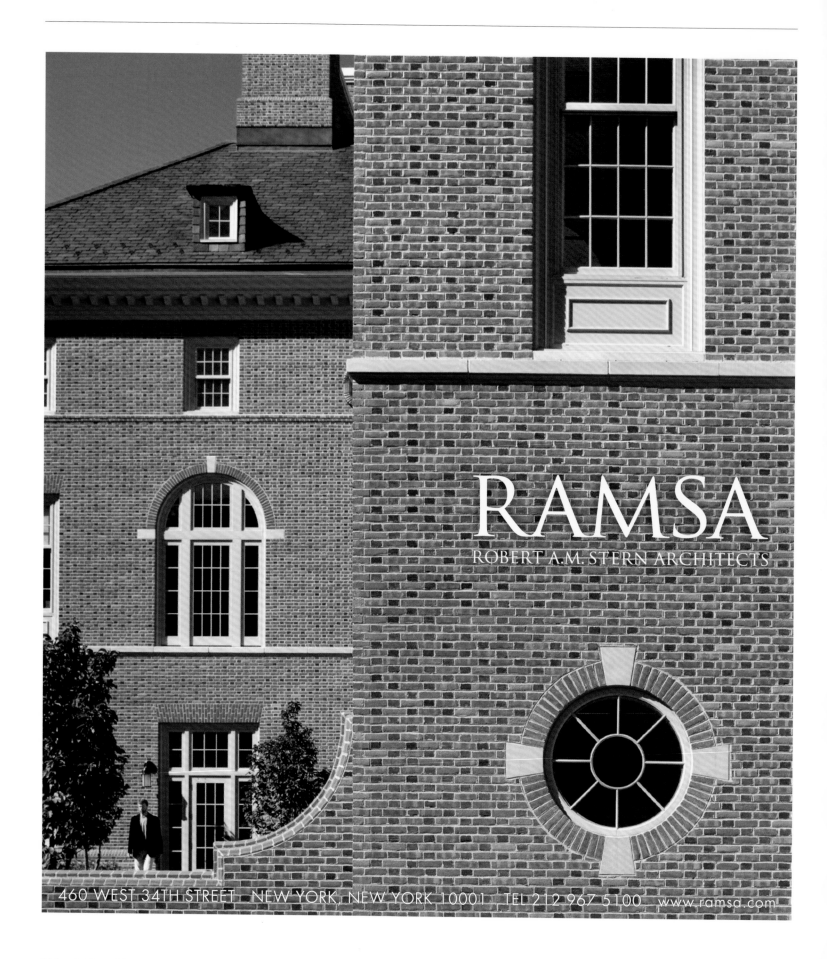

RAMSA
ROBERT A.M. STERN ARCHITECTS

460 WEST 34TH STREET   NEW YORK, NEW YORK 10001   TEL 212 967 5100   www.ramsa.com

VELLA INTERIORS
BUILDERS OF EXQUISITE RESIDENCES

VELLAINTERIORS.COM ~ 718-729-0026
NEW YORK CITY

HENRY FITTINGS
& GROVE BRICKWORKS
DESIGN AUTHENTICITY, QUALITY, AND CRAFTSMANSHIP

HENRY LOW PROFILE DECK MOUNTED LAVATORY FAUCET
WITH LEVER HANDLES AND GROVE BRICKWORKS IN SUGAR WHITE

ESTB. 1978
WATERWORKS

WWW.WATERWORKS.COM | 1 800 899 6757

APPLETON & ASSOCIATES INC - ARCHITECTS
Santa Monica & Santa Barbara, California
www.appleton-architects.com

Architectural Heritage

FINE PERIOD & MODERN GARDEN ORNAMENT,
ARCHITECTURAL ELEMENTS &
BESPOKE STONE FIRE SURROUNDS

Taddington Manor, Taddington, England GL54 5RY
www.architectural-heritage.co.uk
Tel: +44 [0] 1386 584 414

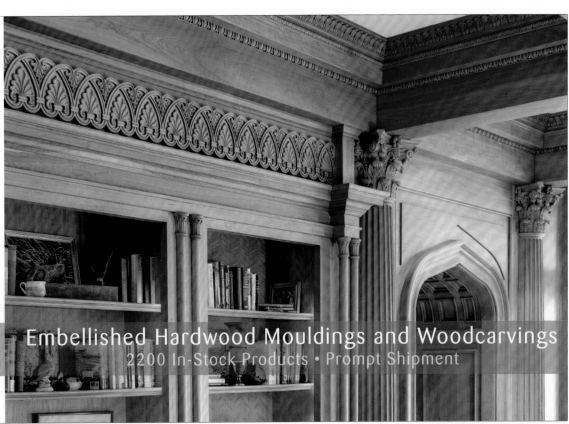

The Institute of Classical Architecture & Art celebrates the wit, wisdom,
and generosity of Paul Gunther during his decade of service as the Institute's President.
With profound gratitude for his devoted stewardship of the ICAA and its mission,
we wish him the very best in all his future endeavors.

❧

Production:
Composed with Quark XPress 9.5 and Mac OS X

Text: Japanese Matte Art 140gsm
Cover: Japanese Matte Art 230gsm
Separations: 300 Line Screen
Printing: Offset Lithography
Binding: Perfect Bound
Edition: 2,500

Typefaces:
Centaur, designed by Bruce Rogers
for the Metropolitan Museum in 1912–14,
based on the Roman type cut in Venice by Nicolas Jensen in 1469,
modified by Dyad Communications.

Trajan, designed by Carol Twombly in 1988,
based on the inscription carved on the pedestal of
Trajan's column Rome, 113 A.D.

❧